THE OUTERMOST FRONTIER

THE OUTERMOST FRONTIER

A German Soldier in the Russian Campaign

by

HELMUT PABST

WILLIAM KIMBER

LONDON

First published in England in 1957 by
WILLIAM KIMBER AND CO. LIMITED
100 Jermyn Street, London SW1Y 6EE

English Translation © 1957
William Kimber and Co. Limited

ISBN 0-7183-0600-7

This edition reprinted 1986

Printed and bound in Great Britain by
Biddles Ltd, Guildford and King's Lynn

PUBLISHER'S NOTE

Early on the morning of 22nd of June, 1941, the German army, with an overall strength of more than three million men, crossed the Russo-German and Russo-Roumanian frontiers. One army group struck north-east, in the direction of Vilna-Leningrad. Another struck south-east towards Kiev and the Ukraine. The third—Army Group Centre, under von Bock—advanced due east in the direction Bialystok-Minsk-Smolensk-Moscow.

Attached to an artillery unit within this army group was a thirty-year-old Signals N.C.O., Helmut Pabst, formerly a law student and a veteran of the German occupation of France. From the first week of the Russian campaign Pabst kept a diary in the form of letters to his parents and friends in Frankfurt-on-Main, and particularly to his father, who had served in the Russian campaign of 1914–17.

Writing beneath the shadow of the Field Post censorship, he tells the story of three summers and two winters of bitter fighting, not only with a soldier's eye for feats of arms, but also with a sincere love of the Russian people and, later, profound disgust at the higher conduct of the war. Between the lines one may find an increasing irony, which reaches its conclusion with a disavowal of all the propaganda which an ordinary young German—by no means a Nazi—had unconsciously absorbed under Hitler.

The arrangement of the diary as presented in this book was made by the German literary editor, Mr. Hermann Meyer, who also chose the chapter headings. The occasional passages in italics have been added by the translators to identify certain actions against the general background of the war. The story itself is unretouched and its observations remain unrationalized, for Pabst fell in action in the autumn of 1943.

Translated from the German
by
Andrew and Eva Wilson

CONTENTS

CHAPTER I

THE ADVANCE ON SMOLENSK

IT's hard to believe that it started only two days ago. This time
I was with the leading wave. The units moved up to their
positions quietly, talking in whispers. There was a creaking of
wheels—assault guns. Two nights before, we had looked over
the ground; now we were waiting for the infantry. They came
up in dark, ghostly columns and moved forward through the
cabbage plots and cornfields. We went along with them to act as
artillery liaison unit for the second battalion. In a potato field the
order came "Dig in!" No. 10 Battery was to open fire at 0305
hours.

0305. The first salvo! At the same moment everything sprang
to life. Firing along the whole front—infantry guns, mortars.
The Russian watch-towers vanished in a flash. Shells crashed
down on all the enemy batteries, which had been located long
before. In file and in line, the infantry swarmed forward. Bog,
ditches; boots full of water and mud. Ahead of us the barrage
crept forward from line to line. Flame-throwers advanced against
the strong-points. The fire of machine-guns, and the high-
pitched whip of rifle bullets. My young wireless operator, with
forty pounds' load on his back, felt a bit queasy during the first
half-hour. Then, at Kanopky Barracks, came the first serious
resistance. The company ahead was stuck. "Assault guns, forward!"

We were with the battalion commander on a small hill, five
hundred yards from the barracks. Our first man wounded—one
of the runners. We set up the wireless. Suddenly we were fired on
from close quarters. A sniper. We picked up our rifles for the

first time. Although we were signallers, we must have been the better shots—the sniping stopped. Our first kill.

The advance went on. We moved fast, sometimes flat on the ground, but irresistibly. Ditches, water, sand, sun. Always changing position. Thirsty. No time to eat. By ten o'clock we were already old soldiers and had seen a great deal: abandoned positions, knocked-out armoured cars, the first prisoners, the first dead Russians.

For three hours during the night we stood-to in a foxhole. Tanks were threatening our flank. At a quarter to four we went on again with the infantry. Again we were preceded by a barrage. On either side of us we could see companies fighting forward. Quite close by, flares were going up. We were right in the front line.

The first burnt-down village, with only the chimneys still standing. Here and there a shed, and the usual draw-wells. Under shell-fire for the first time. The shells make a curious singing noise: you dig in fast and make yourself flat. Constant changes of position. We dump our set on the ground. Reception is good, unlike yesterday. But we have hardly taken a message before the battalion moves on. We run after it.

About three o'clock we get through the dugout line, a defile between swamps. Suddenly a halt. Someone calls: "Anti-tank guns, forward!" The guns race through. Then there's a waste of sand, covered with clumps of broom. It extends about two kilometres to the main road and the river, by the fortress of Osowiec.

For breakfast we had a slice of bread. For lunch four of us shared an inch-thick crust. Thirst, heat, and this damned sand! We trot along wearily, taking the carrying in turns. Splashed, muddy, sand in our boots, two-day-old beards. Battalion headquarters at last, at the edge of the plain. Up by the river is our most forward post. The Russians know exactly where we are.

We dig in quickly. God knows, we're none too soon. We already know exactly when a shell's coming, and I can't help laughing when we dive headlong into our holes and crouch there like Muslims at prayer. But at last it gets too much of a good thing: the infantry pull back. We dismantle the set and make a dash whenever there's a lull in the firing. There are others running on our right and left and we all flop down in the mud at the same time. I can't stop laughing.

When we reached comparative safety, we gathered in a fox-hole and waited for darkness. We shared our last cigarettes. The mosquitoes went quite mad. More signals came in. I almost went crazy decoding them, because my torch attracted more mosquitoes still. Again there were infantry coming back from the front line. We weren't quite certain what was going on.

A hill, a deep trench—we knew we must be somewhere. There was soup, and coffee—as much as we wanted. After going on two more kilometres through the dark we ended up at one of our batteries. Soon we were lying close together, pulling our jackets round our ears. The Russian shells were wishing us good night. When we crept out again at about four o'clock, we found ourselves a hundred yards from our headquarters.

An hour later we were marching west, then north. When night fell we were near Augustova, whose church with its two towers reminded me of Father. A bit beyond Augustova, in the direction of Grodno, we were put at readiness again. We had to be ready at half-past ten. We were woken up at half-past twelve, and eventually we started at five o'clock in the morning. The situation was changing all the time; the front was moving forward very fast. We marched towards Grodno, where we were to be used. Swamps left and right of us. A whole Russian tank brigade was supposed to be somewhere on the right, but one never gets to see such things. (Only mosquitoes—there are enough of those, and dust.)

Finally, in the evening, we got into a village by country tracks that took us through Lipsk. Everywhere pillars of dust were

13

rising in the air and moving slowly with the columns along the roads.

The road to Kutnitza is a torrent of sand. It's all beaten down, rutted and full of craters. It pours downhill like an arid sea. Painfully we push across the slopes, sometimes winding in serpentines. Perhaps it was like that in Napoleon's campaign. At night we halt somewhere in the sand desert. It's cool and it's raining. We creep under the vehicles, shivering. In the morning we go on, dirty and dusty and streaked with rivulets of sweat. Kutnitza. The narrow road by which we march in is flanked by three cemeteries—Catholic, Orthodox and Jewish. The first Orthodox church with its onion-shaped towers. In the meantime we've exchanged the monotonous plain for a charming park-like landscape. There are gardens round the houses, modest attempts at beauty, some ornament on the buildings and fruit trees.

The place is partly destroyed. There's a whole block burnt down. In one house there is still the kitchen range and a piece of chimney. A man and woman crouch before it, and the range is smoking. An old man in a fur coat sits barefoot on a stool, grinning at us happily. His schnapps-reddened nose shines in the wild scrub of his beard.

An hour later we reached a decent hard road, bound for N. The light artillery joined up with us; the horses and guns approaching over a crest looked like a paper cut-out. Not too warm. A gently undulating plain, and no dust. A wonderful morning. The thatched wooden houses might have been decrepit, but the village church stood white and shining on a hill, a visible token of its power.

This marching is more strenuous than action. An hour and a half's rest from one-thirty to three. Later we marched with the moon behind us into a dark, threatening sky. It was like marching into a dark hole; the ghostly landscape was pale and bare. We slept like the dead for an hour and got up unsteadily with an awful pressure in the stomach. A delicate morning. Pale, fine colours. You wake up slowly, and at each stop you sleep. At any time during these advances you can see troops sleeping by the wayside, just as they have thrown themselves down. Sometimes they're doubled up like dead, or else they're like a couple of motor-cyclists I saw this morning, happily out on their backs beside each other, in greatcoats and steel helmets, with their legs apart and their hands in their pockets.

The thought of having to get up penetrates your drugged sleep with difficulty. It took me a long time. When I woke the man next to me, he kept falling back with a completely blank face. I found another one, who had done a guard duty, with a deeply lined face and feverish eyes. Another had started to write a letter to his girl and had fallen asleep. I took the sheet away quietly; he hadn't quite managed three lines.

13th of July, 1941. Move at 1630, just before a thunderstorm. We were sweating horribly. The thunderstorm was a roaring barrage. It's a relief, but the sultriness remains. For four hours we marched at a fantastic pace without stopping. Even after that we were deceived each time we halted; we went on almost at once. At nightfall there was three-quarters of an hour's rest.

Night. From the hill where we stood we could see a number of fires far on the horizon. At first I thought it was the dawn. The yellow dust hung about like fog, moving lazily sideways or veiling the shrubs beside the track.

When the sun came up like a red ball, we had a problem on our hands. In the half-light our Air O.P. wireless cart—a high-wheeled monstrosity which was once a French ration wagon—had run off the corduroy road. A horse had done a somersault in the traces, and two others, which were led down the embankment to clear the road, had got stuck in the bog and entangled themselves in the field trunk wire. Hell broke loose. With fresh horses and another pair to help them, we got the wagon out of its precarious position and hurried after our unit.

We found them sooner than we expected, a few kilometres further on, in a wood beside a lake. The whole wood was one big troop and ammunition depot, crammed to the last square inch. We warmed up our lunch and pitched the tent; and as we crawled inside, it started to rain. Through a small rent in the canvas the rain fell on my face, but the weather was still so close that it did me good. Besides, I was very tired. In the morning I went down to the lake. The water was warm. I had time to wash my underwear, which was now getting rather field grey.

16th of July. Move at 1400 hours. We marched till our knees were shaking, as far as L. It was terribly close, and our thirst was awful. In the village one of our horses lost a shoe. A thunderstorm broke and I stayed behind with the others to look for a farrier in one of the batteries marching behind. Our own smithy had stopped in the rear to repair the limber of our field kitchen, which had a broken back axle.

We found a farrier. Some of the boys gave us bread, tea, cigarettes and cigarette paper, and we rode into the gathering dusk and another thunderstorm. The horses kept shying, unable to make out the road. Finally, an hour later, we came on the dark shadows of guns on the side of the road—stragglers from the unit. In the rain, dark forms were crouching on the vehicles or lying underneath in strange-looking heaps. I found my riders lying all together under the trees. They were sound asleep with the horses hanging their heads close by. Between five and six in the morning we moved to a rest area in a meadow above a village. Reveille at noon, move at four o'clock. Four hours' marching in wet boots. Towards evening it got cool. The road rose and fell through the monotonous landscape, and from far away came the sound of firing. There were bomb craters beside the road. Towards 2200 we turned off onto a patch of grass.

It's cold and wet with a nasty wind. We've gathered wet hay and put up the tent. Somebody has a candle. Now that we've crept inside it's suddenly quite pleasant: four men sitting comfortably under cover round a friendly warm light. Somebody said: "We won't forget this evening," and we all agreed.

20th of July, 1941. Today it's four weeks exactly. Since crossing the German frontier we have done about 800 kilometres; since Kulm 1,250. On the night of the 18th the exact distance from the cross roads in Stahnken, where we formed up in the direction of Grajewo and Osowiec, was 750 kilometres. I'm sitting on a bench by a crossing-keeper's cottage. We're waiting for the rest of the unit to make the difficult crossing of the Duna, which took our little group on horseback more than an hour. The one-way eight-ton emergency bridge can't take all the traffic. At the bottom of the steep bank swarms of prisoners are helping to build a second bridge. Barefoot civilians are scrambling laboriously over the wreckage of the old one, which blocks the little river. The crossing may take hours; there are a hundred and fifty prisoners to give a hand with the pushing.

The town of Vitebsk is completely in ruins. Traffic lights hang like bats in the torn tramway wires. A huge cinema advertisement is still smiling from a fence. The population, mostly women, move cheerfully among the ruins, looking for charred timber for a fire or for any remaining loot. In the suburbs some streets are undamaged, and now and then a little hut has remained intact as if by a miracle. Some of the girls are quite smartly dressed, though sometimes they wear a coat and handbag while walking barefoot with a bundle on their back. There are peasants in from the country with their tiny pony traps; they have sheep-skin coats or linen smocks, and the women wear kerchiefs on their heads. In the suburbs you see the proletariat; lounging adolescents and brazen-faced women. Sometimes you are struck by someone with a finely sculptured head, and then you notice his poor clothing.

The order to continue our line of march was cancelled at the last moment. We halted and loosened the harnesses. Then just as we were about to feed the horses a quarter ration of oats, a new order came. We had to start immediately, double-quick time! The river-crossing was kept clear for us. We marched back, at first going south in the general direction of Smolensk. It turned out to be a peaceful, if hot and dusty, march of only eighteen kilometres. But after the easy day before I found the strain and fatigue made me lose all feeling for the charm of the landscape. Ours is the infantry division which has pushed furthest east; indeed, we marched night and day, and we're still marching.

You see the gentle waving of the cornfields, the scented fields of clover, and in the villages the huddles of thatched, weather-worn cottages, a white church towering over, which has meanwhile been used for other purposes and nowadays may house a field bakery. You see the population queueing at our bakery for bread under the direction of a smiling soldier. You see the questioning eyes of the prisoners who are working everywhere on the roads and bridges, and the peasants who take off their caps when you look at them sharply. You see it all, but only in a half-dream.

At 0200 I woke the advance party, and half an hour later the whole mob. At half-past four we were off. Now it's a quarter-past five in the afternoon on the 26th of July. I am lying sweaty and dusty on the roadside at the bottom of a hill. From here we have to cover a longish stretch of exposed road. There's a rumbling in the distance. Since Surash there's been a lot of air activity, whole wings of Stukas flying against the enemy with their fighter escorts. Yesterday three Russian bombers wheeled over our lake after unloading their stuff a few kilometres away. Before they vanished we saw our fighters hissing on their tails, and machine-guns crackled in the hot noon-day air.

A few days ago we were meeting more and more refugees, then the roads got quieter and we passed the reception camps with a thousand to twelve hundred prisoners. Here there's nothing but the front line. In the villages a great many houses have been abandoned. The peasants who stayed behind draw water for our horses. We take onions and small yellow turnips from their gardens and milk from their churns. Most of them part with it amiably.

We continued along the road with intervals between us. Far ahead, on the edge of a wood, we could see the mushrooms of shell-bursts. We turned off before we got there, into a moderately good sandy track, which turned out to be endless. Night came. Northwards the sky was still light; to the east and south it was lit by two burning villages.

Overhead, bombers were searching for targets and dropping their bombs by the main road behind us. My riders were rocking and swaying on their horses. At half-past three we moved into a limber position; at four our wagon went on to the command post. Now it is seven, and I am lying here a little behind it with two wireless sections in readiness.

A peaceful afternoon. We woke up and ate, slept again and were then put on the alert. It was a false alarm and we went on sleeping. Down through the meadow captured Russians are being escorted to the rear. In the evening light everything looks so friendly. It's been a lovely day. At last we have a little time to ourselves. It's war with intervals. No decisive movements. An anti-tank gun or a tank opens fire; we reply with mortars. The gun makes an ugly sighing sound. Then after a few shells there's quiet. Our batteries plaster an enemy observation post, and the Russians drop a few packets on us. We munch our bread and duck when the music starts. You can hear beforehand exactly where it's coming. Up on the hill the Adjutant calls: "Tanks attacking on Three Company front, sir!"—"Pass to artillery!" answers the Captain, and he calmly finishes shaving.

About three-quarters of an hour later tanks came against us in masses; they were so close that they could sweep the back of our hill. Things got pretty hot. Two O.P.s dismantled and withdrew, the detachment command post and battalion headquarters stayed on. In the meantime our infantry have advanced against the burning village again. I'm lying in a hole up on the hill. In

19

situations like this it's always gratifying to see what divides the wheat from the chaff. Most people are scared. Only a few keep cheerful, and those are the ones who count.

30th of July, 1941. Since last night we've been able to see the signal flares of our people about twenty kilometres away. The ring round Smolensk is contracting. Things have become quieter.

Largely due to the slowness of the German infantry over difficult country, a substantial number of Russians had, in fact, escaped from this "ring". These helped to build a defence line on the Desna, thus giving the German advance its first real check.

Over the way the Russians are burning down their villages; there were fires all night. Since noon today we've been able to see the dirt spouts from heavy shells. An army corps is fighting its way from south to north. The enemy is putting up a desperate defence; the shells are whistling in the wood again. Late in the afternoon we got ready to change our position, moving east. The pocket seems to be breaking up. When it got dark, we came down from our hillside and rolled twelve kilometres eastwards on the autobahn. It's a wide, well-kept road, decorated with the wreckage of tanks and trucks. We are going right through the middle of the pocket, towards the new front, which is already visible on the horizon.

We marched all through the night. Two burning villages painted a gentle reflection on a slate-grey cloudbank, torn all the time by the brutal lightning of explosions. All night long there was a low rolling sound. Then towards morning the cloudbank changed to a pale mauve. The colours had a strange beauty. Slowly we got the sleep out of our bones and became usable again. We took off our steel helmets and coats. In two hours we must be ready for action; the attack is planned for 0600.

1900. The end of a lively day. In a small sector you can never get the general picture, but it seems that the Russians had momentarily cut our supply road and were putting quite a lot of pressure on our flank. In any case, we retreated quickly along the road, which had been so quiet before. Close ahead, we saw the hits of our batteries, which were raking a hillside and village with ricochets, impact and delayed-action fuses. At the same time the shells of the infantry guns were whistling from every side. When we had parked our vehicles in a hollow, we went to the edge of a little wood which was packed with staff officers. Even there it was better not to raise one's head unnecessarily.

At times like that I'm not curious. You never see anything, and in any case it didn't matter to me how far they'd broken into our flank. I knew that when they came within range we could still have a word with each other. Till then I gathered wild strawberries and lay on my back with my steel helmet on my face, a position which offers you excellent sleep and maximum cover. We were a few yards from the General and our Divisional Commander. It's amazing in what positions senior officers may find themselves on a fluid front like this.

Meanwhile our infantry are combing the wood ahead of us. Our tanks are attacking the Russian tanks, scout planes are flying over the lines, and the artillery is preparing a way for the infantry. Three Russian planes managed to bomb our positions half an hour ago, but our fighters got on to them, and they can't have got very far.

To tell the events of 4th of August won't be so easy, particularly as we're on the march.

I was called by the sentry and told to work with the wireless section of No. 7 Company. A sergeant and three men went to find the company. They were in the next village, and we moved off with them. The only difference was that the infantrymen were wearing light battle order, while we had our instrument packs. It was hot and close. There wasn't much contact with the enemy, and we pressed on six to eight kilometres through grassland and low shrub, ideal country for hide-and-seek. We crossed the "Post Road". Two kilometres further on we were fired on from a small wood which had been reported clear. A lively action began. Nebelwerfers, anti-tank guns and a couple of assault guns went into action. Four Russian tanks appeared, of which three got quickly knocked out. One of them came into our left flank from the village of Leshenko and kept us busy for some time. We were with the company commander in a little hollow and were being sniped, so that we couldn't show our noses above cover. There were cries of "Enemy tank ahead!" From the left came the Russians' "Hurrah!" It sounds weird, this battle-cry, and it's an awkward business when you don't know what's happening five hundred yards away. You're all ears, listening to the rise and fall of noise, detecting the difference between friendly machine-guns and the enemy's. The Russian machine-guns have a dull coughing sound, while ours make a high whipping noise.

The attack was repulsed and we tried to make contact with our control. Up to then communication had been fine; now it was suddenly interrupted. We were sitting too low in our hollow. Since we couldn't go higher, we had to give it up. Night fell with some shooting still going on. We couldn't go back, because the road to the rear was uncertain. We stayed on and looked at the burning village of Leshenko.

The fire, which had been started by our own people, was whirling and racing to such effect that still more Russians came out when their seats started to get toasted. It's a brutal way, but one can't do anything else. Incidentally, from now on the fighting became visibly more embittered and merciless on our side too; and only those who were there will understand why. The night brought two more incidents, which cost us two dead and one man badly wounded. Now I know the meaning of the word "frightfulness".

In the morning we woke up to find sweet stillness. Not a shot. Not a sound. Coffee came up, and the switchboard operator was just telling the boys at the O.P.: "We haven't seen a plane yet, and the artillery's leaving us alone——" when there was a hiss and bang, and the first packet fell about two hundred yards to the right. The lieutenant swore, as if the unsuspecting operator had drawn the Russians' attention to us—and we laughed. Since then it's been quiet, hardly a shot, except at midday when I went to the road to show the ration carriers the way to the new command post. Just then our old friend the tank pelted the neighbourhood. There was an ugly red flame in the darting black smoke, and a lot of banging.

It's odd. As soon as we get into a new action and hear the thunder of the guns, we become happy and carefree. Every time it's happened our gang has begun to sing and be gay and in good spirits. There's a new smell of freedom in the air. They're good lads, who love danger, even if they won't admit it.

From time to time a round is fired by one of the batteries. It sounds like a ball thrown very high in the air. You hear it fly further. Then, some time after the rushing sound has ended, you hear the distant dull sound of its impact. The Russian shells have quite a different sound, as if somebody had slammed a door. This morning there was lively firing somewhere in the distance, but otherwise it has been so peaceful since yesterday that you might think you were making a mistake. Perhaps the Russians have realised how senseless their attacks are; perhaps they are watching our supply roads to make a surprise attack in our rear. We can wait. We can observe it all quietly, just as we do their trench digging, which is supposed to defend the approach to Byely. It's an odd war.

Last night I went up as a relief with Arno Kirchner. It takes a good hour from the command post to the O.P. There was a light mist hanging among the trees, and the grass and hedges were heavy with rain. We groped along the path by hollows and slopes down to Monastyrskoje. There was the road. A ghostly silence everywhere. The front was completely quiet except for an occasional shivering flare going up, lonely and chalk-white in the mist which deadened all sound.

23

In the village there were little slivers of light from the cellars and dugouts; somewhere a furtive cigarette, the silent sentry shivering with cold. It was late, towards midnight. The puddles in the shell-holes reflected the stars. Hadn't all this happened before, I thought. Russia, Flanders, front-line soldiers . . .? Sometimes a scene strikes you like that. You think: it must have been like this in the earlier war. It's the same now—timeless.

We were in a hurry and only called out a few words to each other to point out the craters. Spokes and wheels in a ditch, the remains of a local cart. "Direct hit," said Arno drily. What else could you say? It was a devil of a road, leading straight to the enemy in Byely.

"Careful, we must be near the crossing; then there's another fifty yards." We groped through cables and communication trenches.

Finally, there was our man with the wireless, and the hand-set ten yards beyond. The boys were standing round freezing, chest deep in the wet foxholes, with groundsheets round their shoulders. I passed on the order for the telephonists to dismantle; we changed the wireless and I tried to make contact.

I slid into the wet hole, whose worn and soggy walls were lined with rotten straw, and found a narrow place that was dry. It took some skill to get into it legs first. Halfway down the ceiling had collapsed; the side walls weren't thick enough to stand the vibration. It was very cramped. I stuffed my steel helmet and gas mask under the two lowest beams as a precaution, but as the hole was narrower at the bottom than at the top, the danger of being buried alive wasn't very great. True, the ceiling crumbled whenever somebody walked through the trench, but I pulled my blanket over my head and after listening once more to what was going on outside fell quietly asleep.

CHAPTER II

THE SWORD ABOVE THE CALM

While the Panzer forces of the Southern Army Group had encircled and captured 600,000 Russians at Kiev, and the Northern Group was bombarding Leningrad, September found Army Group Centre preparing to resume the advance on Moscow. The main attack was launched on 2nd of October, and resulted in the capture of a further 600,000 Russians at Vyazma. The way to Moscow now seemed open. Pabst's unit appears to have been part of the German 9th Army, which was covering the left flank of the 4th Panzer Army. The latter advanced 50 miles north-eastwards in the rough direction of the capital, and then suddenly struck north towards Kalinin.

IN the morning it started to rain, and it was still raining when we moved off at one o'clock. A fine drizzle from low clouds, the landscape grey and misty, like the Westerwald used to be in autumn sometimes. We plodded over wet grassland and boggy tracks with our two vehicles. Somewhere we found the battery again and the long convoy moved painfully forward. The vehicles were slipping and sliding. They sank in and got stuck. A gun-carriage broke into a foxhole and it was still there next morning.

When it got dark we found dugouts of a sort, belonging to a temporary command post. There we crept about trying to install ourselves. By the time we'd finished our coats were stiff with wet sand and clay. We'd found a dugout with an entrance the size of a rabbit warren's. I groped my way inside and felt a recess lined with straw. My hand touched someone's belt. I thought: This will do me fine. Then I stowed the equipment in various other recesses, and when I came back a little later there was a light in the dugout.

It shone out comfortingly into the rain from a narrow window. Inside, I found two signallers from No. 12 Battery, who had installed themselves the day before. There were three in our own party, and there were only four sleeping places. There was no room to move in this den, every space was crowded out with our wet clothing and equipment. But what did it matter? A roof, a candle stump, a cigarette, and where there are enough of you, you soon get warm.

One man tipped the water out of his boots and the other got ready to go on guard. Antemann and I piled into a bunk together, one with his head to the west, the other with his head to the east. We couldn't turn; we'd fitted ourselves together too cunningly for that. Yesterday we spent all day repairing the damage which this last march did to our equipment and weapons.

But we had a peaceful evening. We stood outside our dugout like a farmer at his gate, till the rain drove us in. Our corner here is still quiet, but on the flank, a little to the south, there's quite a bit of heavy-calibre shelling from time to time. The Russians are using long-range guns there. You put your hands in your pockets and observe it rather like the farmer looking at his potatoes and saying with a professional air: "Coming on quite nicely."

There's nothing heroic about all this. The word shouldn't be misused. We aren't "heroes". The question is, are we even brave? We do what we're told. Perhaps there are times when you hesitate. But you go all the same, and you go " unflinchingly ". That's to say, you don't show anything. Is that being brave? I wouldn't say so.

It's no more than you'd expect; you owe it to yourself not to show fear or, what's more, not to have any. After all, there's no situation which a clear, calm mind can't master. Danger is only as great as our imagination. And because the thought of danger and its consequences only makes you unsure of yourself, it's essential to self-preservation not to let imagination get the upper hand. For days on end, and often for weeks, not a single bullet or shell fragment comes close enough for us to hear it whistle. At such times we peacefully fry our potatoes, and even in the rain (which is just now drumming on our roof) the fire doesn't go out. But even when the whistling comes rather close, there's still a lot of room between the bullets and shells. As I say, you only want to keep calm and watch out.

Father understood this very well. I'm always happy when I read his letters, and it warms my heart to feel that he understands all this from his own war experiences.

It's not really so bad, is it, Father?

Of course, we're up against different weapons, but we have different ones ourselves. A tank can be awkward, if you only have your rifle. But if it comes to the worst, you can always squeeze into a hollow and let it pass. And even a brute like that isn't invulnerable to a single man—provided you get it from behind. But to do that of one's own free will—that's what I'd call brave.

On the whole, war hasn't changed. Artillery and infantry still dominate the battlefield. The increased fire-power of the infantry —automatic weapons, mortars and all the rest—it's not so bad as it's supposed to be. But you have to accept the basic fact, you're after the other man's life. That's war. That's the trade. And it isn't so difficult. Again, because the weapons are automatic, most people don't realise the full implications of it: you kill from a distance, and kill people you don't know and don't see. Situations in which soldier confronts soldier, in which you can say to yourself "That's my man!" and fire, are possibly more common in this campaign than in the previous ones. But they don't happen that often.

22nd of September, 1941. It's between eight and nine in the evening. We're sitting in the dugout. It's so hot that I've stripped to the waist. Our fire's burning high and bright and giving out an enormous heat. It's our only light.

We are all sitting on the bench, writing-pads on our knees, thinking lovingly of home—Heinz of his wife, who's expecting a baby, and I of you, dear parents and friends. We want you to know that we're doing fine, really and truly fine, and that for a little while we're absolutely happy, because we know that we couldn't possibly be better off under the circumstances.

It's all our own work—the bench, the beds, the hearth; and the wood which we tore off a collapsed roof and brought here to put on the fire. We have carried in water, dug potatoes, grated some onions and hung the mess tins over the fire. You provided the cigarettes, the cook-house produced the coffee and the lieutenant gave us this rest break. We've joined all together in a harmonious whole and made a small feast.

Heinz is sitting by the fire, and I'm by the music which comes from the wireless. He too has shed his last clothes. He's sweating like a roast, and we grin at each other whenever we pause in our writing, or look at the fire, or reach for our mugs. What do we care if it rains or blows outside, if they shoot with 150s or 210s: we're warm and snug, as safe as it is possible to be safe; and nobody is likely to call us out. All quiet on the eastern front. Operations are running according to plan. Let them run, old man, we won't run after them, not tonight.

When I got up in the morning there was hoar-frost everywhere. I found thick lumps of ice in the watering bag. Winter isn't far off.

The last day of September. We're in a thoughtful mood; it's deepened by hearing a passage of string music. The fire is dancing brightly. We've hung up our earphones any old where, on the knots of roots and on rifle sights. The violins are everywhere.

The chimneys are smoking in all the dugouts. It's a proper village which climbs up a little valley. The dugouts have been cut into the slope on either side. You go into them at ground level, and there's the width of a narrow street between the two rows. A single vehicle can just about park there, and generally it's our ration cart—a pony and trap. When it arrives the men creep out of their holes, and the village comes to life. Not that it's so very quiet normally during the day, what with the boys cutting wood and fetching water, or coming back from their foraging expeditions to the potato field; nor in the evenings, when they hang about smoking and talking, or carry the latest rumour from dugout to dugout, or crowd round somebody who's come up with the latest news.

What news there is we piece together like bits of a mosaic. Somebody has seen the tanks, the yellow ones which were meant for Africa. Now they've turned up here. Someone else has seen assault guns. And a man from the Nebelwerfers appeared by mistake. All kinds of special weapons—lots of them—guns of every calibre; they are all being concentrated in this sector. It's piling up inexorably like a thunderstorm. It is the sword above the calm—the drawing of breath for a stroke which may be bigger than any we have seen yet.

We don't yet know when it will start. We only feel the veil over the calm getting thinner, the atmosphere gathering tension, the approach of the hour when it will only need a word to let loose hell, when all this concentrated force will spring forward, when the barrage will again be before us and I may be following the machine-guns again. In any case, this is where we shall have to crack the nut, and it will be some crack.

2200 hours. News on every wavelength. I've switched off the wireless to look into the fire for a while, watching the ever fascinating play of the flames. My two comrades fell asleep over the music. It's very quiet, only the fire is alive, and I've taken an ember to light one of my Gauloises which arrived today from Paris. The boys begged me to give them one. "At last a cigarette which still has tobacco in it," remarked one. And the other said: "It reminds you of France."

France. . . . How long ago it was, and how wonderful. What a difference between these two countries, between these two wars! And between them lies a middle-land to which we hope to go back one day. Have I had enough?—No. What has to be, must be. We have to push on with all our energy.

29

Perhaps we shall get a few weeks' rest afterwards. It's not this present kind of rest which we need. It's all right as long as you're just a soldier who's adapted himself to the simplest needs like eating and sleeping. But there's another part of us which wakes up at night and makes us restless—all of us, not just me.

0600. I jump on top of a dugout. There are the tanks! Giants rolling slowly towards the enemy. And the planes. One squadron after the other, unloading their bombs across the way. Army Group Centre has launched its attack.

0610. The first Nebelwerfer salvo. Dammit, it's really something worth seeing; the rockets leave a black trail, a dirty cloud which drifts slowly away. The second salvo goes off! Red and black fire, then the projectile emerges from the cone of smoke. You can see it clearly as soon as the rocket burns off: the things fly straight as arrows through the morning air. None of us have seen it before. Reconnaissance planes come flying back low over the lines. Fighters are circling overhead.

0645. Machine-gun fire ahead of us. It's the infantry's turn.

0820. Tanks roll by, close to the gun position. A hundred have gone by already, and they're still coming on. Where there was a field fifteen minutes ago there's now a road. Five hundred yards to our right assault guns and motorised infantry come on without a pause. The divisions which were lying to our rear are now rolling through us. No. 2 Light Battery changes position and crosses the path of the tanks. The tanks halt, then move on again. It looks like chaos, but it works to the minute, like clock-work. Today they want to break into the Dnieper-line, to-morrow it'll be Moscow. Armoured scout cars are joining the columns. The Russians are firing only sporadically now. It's the same picture over on our left: motor-cycle riflemen and tanks. The assault rolls on; it's far bigger than the one on the frontier defences. It'll be some time before we see a picture like this again.

0905. The main body is through; the only movement still going on is on our right. A few shells land on the hill ahead. A big fellow comes humming towards us, taking a long time to come down as they all do. I shout at one of our drivers, but he just gapes stupidly. A moment later it bursts behind him. He doesn't know what's happened and makes such a funny face that we can't help laughing.

0945. By now I think we've seen the last come by. It's getting quieter. There were 1,200 tanks, not counting assault guns, on a front of two kilometres. Any war film would pale by comparison. "That was really some show!" the boys are saying.

A short while ago the advanced O.P. of Ten Battery sent word that the second line of fortifications had been penetrated. For twenty minutes now we've had no more shelling here. They've fired for the last time. . . . We're standing in the bright morning sunshine warming ourselves. The wireless traffic is going perfectly. Just the right weather for an offensive.

1000. Our first task completed. I lie sheltered from the wind on the empty ammunition boxes, waiting for the new O.P. to be selected so that we can change position. Everybody gathers in a group to chat and smoke. The medical sergeant, Lerch, comes back from the forward area; a signaller in our advanced O.P. has been shot in the thigh. Lerch tells us that up there the ground's all mined, our sappers are winkling them out by the hundred. There are deep trenches and wire. Not many prisoners.

1230. First change of position. So this is the defence line we were plastering. A system of trenches, a stretch of scarred earth, one crater after another. The dead look horribly mangled. There are white tapes giving warning of mines—and the warning's not idle, as we can see from the stacks of mines which did not get laid. The columns move forward through mushrooms which every now and then spring up suddenly from the Russian long-range guns. Or perhaps the mushrooms are mines which we're blowing up: it's difficult to distinguish between the two kinds of bang. Above the troops on the march fly the formations of bombers; then the fighters, swift and silver—Eastward, ho!

1600. The old story again: the change of position has turned into a march. I'm writing this during a rest on the roadside, chewing a piece of bread. It's the same old picture: the wide undulating country, the columns of smoke on the horizon. And again, as before, we don't know where or when the march will end. And anyway, it doesn't matter. On foot or on horseback we drive on with frequent halts—Eastward, ho!

We marched till it got dark and a yellow moon rose over the hills. We spent a pretty cold night in a barn. By first light we were on the road again. Ice was glistening in the puddles; steam rose from both men and horses, white and shining in the rising sun. The pale colours of first light are very beautiful. Like balls of brass, the tracer shells grope for a solitary bomber, and on the horizon the turquoise of the sky is mingled with the red of a fire.

In the meantime we got news that we were going into action. We had to move into a new position across the hills. Over the lines, Stukas were diving and climbing. Prisoners were bringing in wounded, tanks rolled forward, and the battalion went into action. The artillery liaison unit was responsible for fire support. My ears are singing with the gun-fire, and the throat microphone is pinching the stubble of my beard. I am writing this in a hollow. Crash! Take cover! Our aerial is drawing the fire of some tanks. Just as I was about to take the set lower, Control called: "Objective One taken. Battalion held up by enemy tanks and infantry holding edge of wood. Mortars up!"

We opened fire. There were good targets—infantry, anti-tank guns, and a gun tractor. Some of our tanks were stuck too. Stukas arrived in squadrons and dived into attack. The assault got under way again. The flak boys and the tank people had a rendezvous at our post. The flak was going to advance and join in the ground battle.

We came back hungry and frozen and were quartered in a flax-steeper's shed among wonderful silver-grey flax bales. I

32

spread some out and threw myself into them with bare arms and slept like a god.

Days have passed without anything happening. I've brought myself and my underwear up to standard again. I've also done some writing and reading. What a pleasure it is to have a good book. I have read Eichendorff's *Taugenichts*, a story by Stifter, and some short extracts from Schiller and Goethe.

This is another of the bridges that this war has made between Father's generation and mine—just a small one. The greatest is the experience of war itself. How much better we understand each other now, Father. The gulf has gone which separated us sometimes during the years of my growing up. It's a meeting of our ways which makes me very happy. You spoke of it in one of your letters and I can only confirm what you say. Nothing binds us together more closely than having to endure the same privations and hardships and danger, and, indeed, we've been literally in the same places, like Augustova, Lida and on the Beresina. I've passed through your old battlefields. Now I understand the stories you told me, because I've had the same experiences and I know what four years in Russia must have been like. Experience is the best teacher.

There was a time when I and my generation used to say "Yes", thinking we understood. We used to hear and read about war and get excited, just as the younger generation gets excited when it follows the news today. But now we know that war's quite different from any description, even a good one, and that the essential things can't be communicated to someone who doesn't know it at first hand. Between us, Father, we need only to strike a single chord to bring out all the harmonies, only to dab on a single colour to produce the whole picture. Our communications consist only of cues; communications between comrades. So that's what we have become—comrades.

CHAPTER III

THE ROAD TO KALININ

THE going's good on the frozen roads of this country of hills crowned with villages. But fifty-five kilometres is a lot. It took us from eight in the morning till two a.m. next day. And then we didn't find billets. The few houses in our rest area had been allocated long before. But the boys wormed themselves into the overcrowded rooms, determined to get warm even if it meant standing. I myself got into a barn and managed to sleep till seven. At eight we were on the road again.

Marching on this wintry morning was a sheer pleasure. Clean, sweeping country with big houses. People gaze at us reverently. There are eggs and milk and plenty of hay. Flocks of geese perambulate across the yellow grass. We are their undoing, because our rations aren't getting up and our bakery has long lost contact with us. This morning we walked behind the carts peeling potatoes and plucking chickens and geese. The field kitchen served chicken and rice this evening, and now, for good measure, we've got goose and potatoes cooking in our stove. The billets are amazingly clean, quite comparable with German farmhouses. I picked up a plate and a spoon at lunch-time and ate without the slightest hesitation. Afterwards a look was enough, and the family did our washing-up. Pictures of saints everywhere. The people are friendly and open. It's a surprising experience for us.

On the 13th we were going to do only nine kilometres. A morning walk through small wooded valleys, rather like the Spessart in winter. But the pleasure of reaching our new billets was short-lived. We had hardly unsaddled when the order came to march on. It turned into a long, painful march over frozen and slippery roads. It lasted nearly the whole night. Then we lost

34

the way; we stood tired and cold in the wind, till we kindled some fires and crowded round them. Towards five o'clock the lieutenant went to look for billets in the next village so that we could get a few hours' rest.

Winter hasn't stopped at the prologue. Some of the horses still have summer-shoes and they keep slipping and falling. Even Thea, the last horse of the original team of our wireless-cart, has packed it in. After a lot of trouble and humouring I managed to get her as far as a stable here. Ten Battery got stuck in a bog and finally turned back. Things aren't looking too bright. I don't much like the look of Eleven Battery either.

For us it means a rest day. We've crowded into a little bake-house. The nine of us can hardly move. My boots were still so wet this morning that I could only get into them in my bare feet. The billet is full of lice. Our little Viennese was unwise enough to sleep on the stove last night; he's got them too now—and how! Socks which we put there to dry were white with lice eggs. We've caught fleas—absolute prize specimens. The greasy old Russian, to whom we showed these fauna, grinned with all the gaps in his teeth and scratched himself sympathetically: "Me too —nix good!" For some time now, I've always been the last one still awake and not on duty. I can't sleep so much, and some-times I have to be alone with myself. The ghostly pale light from an electric bulb falls on the dark forms on the floor, on the equipment, clothing and weapons which fill the room. Looked at like that, it's a desolate sight, grey within grey, oppressive like a heavy dream. What a country, what a war, where there's no pleasure in success, no pride, no satisfaction; only a feeling of suppressed fury now and then. . . .

It's raining and snowing. Sometimes we're marching on the road to Moscow, sometimes in the direction of Kalinin. It's idle to mention all the billets we arrived at tired and wet. The general impression has changed though. The country's more densely populated. The villages have a town-like air, with brick buildings, two-storeyed houses and little factories. Most of them have a suburban kind of ugliness. Only the houses from before the First World War are pleasant, with intricate wooden ornamentation on the windows and festoons of wooden lace at the gables. With all this go bold colours: bright green and pink, cobalt blue and vermilion. Quite often there are curtains and indoor plants. I've seen houses furnished with excellent taste, shining with cleanliness, with floors scrubbed white, hand-woven rugs, white Dutch stoves with brass fittings, clean beds, and people dressed plainly but well. Not every house is like this, but many are. The people are generally helpful and friendly. They smile at us. A mother made her small child wave to us from behind a window. Faces crowd the windows whenever we march through. The panes are often of a greenish glass which makes for gothic colours—shades of Goya. In the twilight of these dull winter-days a touch of green or red can have a startling effect.

24th of October, 1941. Since last night we have been in Kalinin. It was a tough march, but we made it. We're the first infantry division here and we arrived ahead of two light brigade groups. We marched up the road which stretches into this bridgehead like a long arm, without much covering on either flank. The bridgehead must be held for strategic and propaganda purposes. The road bears the stamp of war: destroyed and abandoned equipment, tattered and burnt-out houses, enormous bomb craters, the pitiful remains of men and animals.

The town is the size of Frankfurt without its suburbs. It's a haphazard conglomeration, without shape or character. It has trams, traffic lights, modern blocks, hospitals and public buildings —all mixed up with miserable wooden shacks and log-houses. The new flats stand on sandy wastes, never surrounded by anything more than a wooden fence. Next to them lie factory buildings in all their ugliness, with goods sheds and railway sidings. However, for a good hour we rolled over asphalt roads, and we've read fanciful names like "Culinaria" and "Lucullus" over restaurants. We watched the remaining population doing some hurried looting.

The Russians are still in the suburbs; up to two days ago their tanks were still refuelling in the town. They have a dirty trick of racing through the streets and just knocking our own vehicles down. We've had some irritating loses that way. As we marched in, we found they'd ranged their guns on the main road, and they put us into a smart trot. It was quite a circus. All the same, this afternoon eight out of sixteen aircraft which bombed the crowded airfield were shot down. They were flying low and crashed in a short, searing blaze. Once we've relieved the tanks, they'll soon clear us some elbow room.

It's a strange life on this island in a foreign country. We have come to accept anything, no matter how strange, and nothing surprises us any more. For the past quarter of an hour it's been getting lively in the sector on our right. The line to No. 3 Battery is out of action. The line patrol is going out. It's bitterly cold outside.

It's a serious war—serious and sober. It's probably different from what you imagine; less terrible—because for us the things that are supposed to be terrible have not many terrors left. Sometimes we say: "Let's hope it'll soon be over." But we can't conceive that it'll be over tomorrow or the day after. So we shrug our shoulders and get on with the job.

I stood alone in a house and lit a match, and the bugs fell from the ceiling. On the walls and floor regiments of vermin were crawling. By the fireplace it was quite black: a horrible, living carpet. When I stood still, I could hear it rustle and grate unceasingly. Nitchevo—it doesn't upset me any more. I just wonder and shake my head.

2nd of November, 1941. 1600 hours. The Russians attacked all night. Today it's quieter. The trees drip in the fog and the crows shake their feathers. The Russians are reported to be planning a big attack. Silence before the storm. All day yesterday I was down at headquarters getting my boots mended. Towards evening I returned to our position with Franz Wolf. We walked hands in pockets, collars upturned and pipes in our mouths. While we were leisurely plodding along, our belts and everything metal iced up and our collars and caps froze stiff with the cold.

It must have been about half-past three when the Russians laid down a carpet with their damned gun. It fell on the hill in front of us, a sequence of violently flickering sheaves of fire, running right to left at intervals of a fraction of a second. A series of ugly explosions. The sky turned red, and Franz said: "Damn it, that was our village again."

Since I had nothing to do, I took the chance of paying a visit to the wireless section at No. 3 O.P. This meant going towards the fire. When we came to the crest of the hill we started puzzling: had it caught the little house or not? We looked across the crest and Franz said: "Over here they always pick you off from left to right."

He'd hardly spoken when we were both flat on the ground. We laughed our heads off, because not long before Franz had declared he wouldn't do it any more, it was too silly. "It's stronger than you; it's instinct," he said; then as we went on, he continued: "—and over there they shoot at you straight down the village street."

We didn't have to wait long for the machine-guns, and after some rapid crawling we turned right. Meanwhile we'd seen that it wasn't the little house that had caught it, but the barn next door. "That was Zink's cow. He'll have something to say about that."

We walked over patches of grass which had been charred by the multiple gun, and turned into the village street. On the right, Wolf's house was the only one left. It was a neat little building, a brand new commissar's office, with a clean raftered ceiling, a desk and a white Dutch stove. No vermin, of course—nobody had lived there.

Zink was lying on a coloured rug by the wireless set—an exotic sight in the half-light of the oil lamp. And he had something to say all right. The barn had been burning since the first salvo of the day, at half-past twelve. Zink was milking the cow. "It blew me into the hay. After a while I picked myself up. I stared at the cow and the cow stared at me. Then the fire got going, and I untied the cow and took her to safety. Since then I haven't been out all day. Once was enough!"

In the evenings we talk about serious matters; about our situation, our impressions and experiences; about changes in character, about our jobs before the war and those we'll do afterwards; about what is to become of us, of Russia, and of Germany. Then there are jokes, because the motorised boys call us the Hunger Division, always on the spot, without a supply echelon, waifs and strays. . . . We get no new boots or shirts when our old ones wear out: we wear Russian trousers and Russian shirts. And when our boots have had it, we wear shoes and Russian puttees —or else make the puttees into ear-muffs.

But we have our rifles and a bare minimum of ammunition. "Well, look who's here!" say the motorised boys. But we have our answer. "Our General has iron nerves," we say. Willingly or unwillingly, the country feeds us.

Since five this morning it's been snowing again; the wind blows the fine, dry snow through all the cracks. The infanteers protect themselves as best they can, with fur gloves, woollen caps, ear-muffs made from Russian puttees, and quilted trousers. We put our noses outside and fly back to the stove. Pity the poor rifle companies out there in their dugouts and foxholes. This isn't proper position warfare. We're not equipped for it and we have no proper dugouts, although we've been stuck here for some time. We don't mean to be stuck, we've got to go on.

The snow is falling thickly and silently; it no longer blows about so much. It deadens all noise and it blinds you. The occasional shots which come out of the unreal greyness sound hollow. You don't even know why they're firing. Abandoned horses—foals and aged mares—trot through the snow hanging their heads, appearing and disappearing in the solitude.

39

As we walked over the night-shrouded plain towards our quarters on the hill, the wind was blowing crystals of snow down our necks and we didn't talk much. Once Franz said: "It's a god-forsaken country." Then at the crossroads we said goodbye. As we shook hands, we hesitated for a moment . . . and Franz's stooping figure vanished quickly into the darkness. There are times when a picture impresses itself on your consciousness. This was such a time. Taking a last look at my departing friend, I felt detached from the event in which I was participating. We never know where we are going, even if most of the time we laugh about such thoughts.

I have a coat again. Antemann is gone. Another good comrade less. The coat is old, it's seen two campaigns. The collar's greasy and the pockets are out of shape. Just the job for Russia, for someone who wants to bury his hands deep in his pockets and keep his pipe in his mouth; for someone who wants to create a vacuum round himself because he's grown almost indifferent to everything. I feel fine like that. I find pleasure in hardening myself against all these miseries, setting my strength and peace of mind against this dog's life, so that in the end I may profit by it.

We're now twenty-eight men in this room, plus four women and a child. They sleep partly next door in the kitchen, and partly on the stove in here. My own sleeping place by the door is in everybody's path. Because we have a battery radio set, we even have guests in the evening. It creates quite a traffic problem; you can hardly turn round. When the majority have gone to sleep I start writing, and sometimes we play a game of chess while others take off their shirts for the nightly louse hunt. It's then that the infanteers begin to talk, the real foot-sloggers like the machine-gunner or the chap from the rifle company.

It's difficult to describe the talk on an evening like this. There's so much in the atmosphere of it; the way people sit with their elbows on their knees or lean back with folded arms. Of course we're depressed sometimes, but it's not worth talking about, because humour always gets the better of us. For example, we pick up the map and say: "Now, once we get to Kazan. . . ." or "Does anyone know where Asa is?" Today somebody said: "We'll be home for Christmas. . . ."—"He didn't say which year," said someone else with a grin. "Just think of it, you get home and the first thing you know, they nab you for the home guard. . . . Up at five on a Sunday morning, and someone standing there and yelling: 'Machine-gun firing from the left!' or '200 yards beyond village, Russian infantry! What's your action?' "

"You tell them you're going into the village to catch a few chickens for the frying-pan," says Franz. "What else?"

And Zink says: "If somebody wants to talk to me, I'll ask him if he's been in Russia."

Although Kalinin had been taken, the main advance towards Moscow had come to a standstill in the mud and the forests about sixty miles short of the capital. Following a new attempt to reach Moscow on December 2nd, which actually resulted in German troops reaching the outskirts, the Russians launched their first great counter-attack. In a few days the Ninth and Fourth Panzer Armies were forced back 100 miles, and Kalinin had to be abandoned.

1st of January 1942. A Happy New Year to you all! We marched out of the burning village into the night, and everywhere we marched the flames were sweeping skywards, feeding black smoke trails. Now the boys are all asleep. I have just been out to wish my sentries a Happy New Year. "Perhaps it'll see us home," I said.

On the morning of the First it was still more than forty degrees below zero. We bound our boots with rags and watched each other's noses. When the tip of the nose goes white, it's time to do something about it. Franz and I were riding with the advance party. Franz couldn't get into the stirrups because of the rags round his boots. He took off his gloves to undo the wire which held the rags together. Two of his fingers got frost-bitten. A number of us have frost-bitten feet, some of them third degree.

41

The Russians are pressing desperately after us. They are trying at all costs to capture a village intact, but we don't leave them a single one.

On January the 9th we were riding to Lu. to find accommodation for our supply echelon. It was already dark. The narrow trail of a road was only recognisable from branches stuck into the snow. We trotted a distance of four kilometres. The horses kept breaking through the snow, jumping up and scrambling forward with difficulty. It was like riding camels; we swayed and balanced, trying to lift the weight off their front and hindquarters in turn, giving them what help we could. It was a strange cavalcade, the three of us among the shrubs and the hills. Behind us the sky was red again. Occasionally there was gun and rifle fire; otherwise it was very quiet.

There was an icy wind. Since last night it has been driving the snow in banners and ribbons across the countryside. It piles up bridges and dunes over every track, and the roads are under deep drifts. Now we are waiting for our men. They have to come from thirty kilometres away. Will they make it?

2000 hours. Now they can't make it. It's been dark for hours. At half-past four we had already taken our evening meal. We looked at our watches and shook our heads: still so early, yet night had fallen some time before. The air is full of snow, crystals of ice like fine needles, which the wind blows through every crack. The lights on the other side of the village street are shining feebly, and if you venture out the wind tears at your clothes. It's good to stay by the fire.

Thank God for the potato. We weren't prepared for a long stay in these parts, and what would have become of us without it? How could a whole army survive a Russian winter without this humble vegetable? Tonight, as always, we have peeled off the skin, broken it reverently, and sprinkled it with the rough Russian salt.

Now it's morning. We have finished breakfast, and again it

was the potato which has made us feel satisfied. All the house has to offer is potatoes, tea and a bread pie, which is served hot and steaming and is filled with a sticky mixture of rye, barley and onions. Perhaps there were a few brown cockroaches in it; at least, I cut one of them out without saying anything. The saint in the corner looks out mildly from his golden frame, as if to say that a calm spirit can well overlook such trifles. What good would it do to notice them? It could only prevent me from enjoying the glories of creation, which appeared again this morning in all their beauty.

The first ray of sunrise was a skyward pointed line of flaming green and red. Then, in the north-east, there was a strange light: its centre was like molten metal, and it was framed by two arcs of such blinding brilliance that it hurt my eyes to look at them. The country was bathed in a magic golden-white mist, trees and bushes were shrouded in glittering glory, and far in the distance roof-tops and hill-crests shone white against the soft grey of the horizon. In this dawn sounds floated strangely enchanted and intangible, as if it were all a fairy-tale play.

We rode back in bright sunshine; it was my last ride with Franz Wolf and my old comrades. I have been transferred to the Battery. The Signaller is dead: Long live the Gunner!

Ivan has woken up. We gave him a push which penetrated to the top; now it has rebounded and he's on the offensive.

Last night we drove back three patrols on the battalion sector. The last consisted of twenty men. Only one of them fell on our side of the wire. As for the rest, there were many little heaps along the trail in no-man's-land in the morning. One was still smouldering. Perhaps he had been carrying a petrol bomb, and one of our tracer bullets hit it.

During the night the Russians came in with a flame-thrower. During the day it was phosphorus grenades, and in the evening another twenty-man patrol was driven back. Ivan's sending over quite a lot of heavy stuff now. In the cold the explosions are extra loud. The fragments make a shrill, sharp whistle, but the effect isn't very great. We're too well covered. Our heavy mortar shells catch Ivan much worse. They bounce off the ground and explode in the air. That way they achieve the much dreaded ricochet-airburst effect of an artillery shell, against which no trench is safe. When one of our "Stukas-on-foot" strikes, the earth trembles for a kilometre all round.

In one of the companies they're busy building a trench-mortar, with which they mean to throw Teller mines into Ivan's trenches, thirty or forty yards away. Its construction reminds you of a Roman catapult. It's very primitive. Such weapons are the children of trench warfare. When the front starts moving again, they are quickly forgotten. But this playing with toys proves the fighting morale of the unit.

The day before yesterday I took part in my first shoot. Ten rounds. It was a wonderful feeling. You forget everything—the danger, the cold. It's a duel. Actually, we weren't in danger; it was like being on the range. Our first hit was close to a personnel dugout which we'd been watching all day. We fired at two other dugouts. At the third there was a fountain of earth like a mine explosion. It was our farewell shot. Afterwards we pulled back to St., where we were quartered some time ago. From here we are to go to prepared positions.

Yesterday I went over and saw the old gang. Franz has at last got the Iron Cross (First Class). The citation said: "For following an enemy tank at Si. to the next village and trying to knock it out with an anti-tank bullet." We laughed till tears ran down our cheeks. For that, of all things! At the time he'd got a tremendous dressing down. All the same, I was glad. Old Franz has really earned it. I got there just as the section was falling in. "We miss you," Franz said afterwards. We're a bit ashamed of sentiment, but there's something in it. "The old gang" . . . it's a whole world. Isn't that so, Father?

CHAPTER IV

THE BATTLE ROUND O.P. RED

The failure before Moscow had been accompanied by an equal set-back in the South, where having reached Rostov, "the gateway to the Caucasus", late in November, the Panzer army of von Kleist had been forced to retreat to the river Mius. On the Central Sector the Russian counter-offensive lasted three months and caused some of the most bitter fighting of the war. While the Russians were aided by large numbers of Siberian ski troops, the Germans were without winter equipment of any kind. They managed, however, to establish and hold a line behind the bastions of Rzhev, Vyazma and Briansk. This was on the orders of Hitler, who took over command of the army after Rundstedt's resignation in December. The battle round Observation Post Red and other actions in the following chapters were probably fought near Rzhev, the most northerly of the three bastions, 150 miles west of Moscow.

Today nothing much happened, except that the villages before us were burning, and the sun glowed through the clouds of smoke like a red ball. The refugees—old men, women and children—made their way painfully through the snow. They were dragging small hand sledges and leading cows and dogs. The women's voluminous sheepskin coats hung stiffly down their bodies; their bundles and coloured blankets shone brightly, and the old men with their frosted beards looked like Father Christmases. Towards evening the fires turned blood-red; now they're shining like evil eyes out of the darkness.

Tonight the infantry will fall back on the prepared positions. The machine-gun nests and pillboxes form an unbroken line, with wire obstacles standing in the snow like toys. The dance can begin. The white dance of death.

Visibility is getting worse. A keen wind is filling the air with snow. As if through veils we can see the Russians coming forward. We're keeping a sharp eye on them; we know what's coming.

25th of January, 1942. 0400. The nights are cold. The snow lies blue under the silver moon, and in the shadows it's as blue as indigo. A hundred yards ahead the machine-gun posts on the steep slope of the gully look like a mountain range on the moon. From time to time a sentry moves, the snow creaks; occasionally there's a burst of firing which echoes and re-echoes for a long time afterwards in the valley of the little river. Every three hours I go up to the O.P. and do an hour's forward watch, and when we fire I stay longer. Sleep comes in snatches; in forty-eight hours I have slept for eight. Not all nights are as quiet as this one.

The sector on our left is a weak spot. The day before yesterday the enemy knocked out a machine-gun there and cleared out a dugout in hand-to-hand fighting. Yesterday, in the same sector, they broke through our line. It happened towards evening. Soon a number of houses in the village were on fire. The enemy pushed on under cover of the smoke. I stood outside listening to their battle-cries. They roar like bulls when they attack. At the same time they tried to come through the gully and attack the village on our right. They were thrown back. For a long time I heard a wounded man crying. Nearly all night they were firing with light artillery. Some of the guns fired tracer fragmentation shells; they travel slowly and crack high overhead showering down whistling splinters. But we did a surprise shoot and our own shells sounded more impressive. They start on a high pitch and end with a deep humming like an organ. When they fly through the air one after another they create powerful chords. Up in front, helping to direct the shoot, you watch the violent lightning, the mighty explosions. Enormous spouts of smoke and snow cover the whole target area. It's like a giant's fist coming down.

I can't deny that I feel proud at moments like that. It's a proud job directing these heavy shells; even if my own part in it is infinitely small, they're "our" shells and it's "our" battery that does the firing. Whenever timber and earth are blown sky-high over there in the enemy lines, or an enemy attack gets bogged down by our firing, the infantry are jubilant; they're happy as snow-devils and they're grateful to us. On our side, we're proud that it went so well. Hunger, cold, fatigue—we forget them all when we are firing.

We knew what was coming. We saw every development with absolute clarity. I made a last dash through the wind and shelling to our flank observation post, a kilometre away in the front line. The enemy had already started firing with tanks and anti-tank guns.

The prelude. How well we knew it!

I found the boys in a forward machine-gun post and shook hands with them. Pfeil shared a slice of toast with me and I gave him one of my last cigarettes. Then I raced back through the wood to make a new track with my skis, along which a new cable was to be laid to the O.P. I moved on a compass bearing, hurrying all the time, and even with the skis I kept breaking knee-deep into the snow. But already it was too late. A few hours later the cable along the firing line had been cut by shells in twenty places, the front between the O.P. and ourselves had been broken, and in this same wood the enemy's signal flares were going up.

In the morning there was no sign of our observers. Later two of them came back. One stayed behind, there had been a direct hit. We didn't sleep that night, our dugout became a report centre for six units. Runners kept coming and going. Most of them didn't bring very good news: "Lieutenant von H. has been killed in hand-to-hand fighting; we didn't see the Russians till they were five yards away . . ."—"The dugouts are falling one after another. . . ."

All the time we had to keep asking for more sledges for the wounded. They came through the back of the wood, along our cable, which they were constantly tearing. Our line patrol had to be out all night.

On the 28th the Russians made their first break-through on our right. They threw the next company out of their positions and occupied P., which stands on a prominent hill and cuts into our flank like a wedge. We did a shoot with anti-tank guns and set some houses on fire; and a mob of bakers, butchers and medical orderlies was rounded up hastily to seal off the gap. But our sledge road through P. had been cut. Only the foot track through the wood was left.

Counter-attacks have all failed. Night after night we have fired concentrations to wipe them out. Night after night the infantry have gone into the attack, after being in the open in this terrible cold since the 27th. They knew full well that the effort was hopeless. For the third time P. was to be taken at all costs. "The front-line dugouts will be re-occupied. Any man leaving his post will be court-martialled and shot." The mood in our dugout is extremely sombre.

The commander of our infantry company comes from an old family—Lieutenant von Hindenburg. Strain has drawn rings under his eyes. In moments when he thinks he's not being watched, a great tiredness overtakes him and he grows quite numb. But as soon as he takes the receiver in his hand, his quiet, low voice is clear and firm. He talks to his platoon commanders with such convincing warmth and confidence that they go away reassured. His own courage is self-sufficient, he wears it as naturally as his uniform.

Soon it will be zero hour. Slowly I am getting ready. Lieutenant von Hindenburg has meanwhile gone to sleep. His job is finished. He'll sleep soundly till the first runners arrive.

Shortly afterwards I was at the O.P. waiting for the artillery concentration which was to precede the attack. The night was dark blue like a starless vault over the light landscape. The snow reflected a gentle red from the fires in P. We watched the bombardment. It came down at a single blow, the ricochets jumping like gargoyles over the roofs.

That night a platoon of Pioneers—an officer and forty-two men—did an attack. Eleven killed, nine seriously and seven lightly wounded. The officer came back ashen-faced with fifteen men.

Next morning the way to our O.P. was scarcely passable. We were under fire from the dugouts which the Russians had captured, as well as from P. An anti-tank gun had ranged on us so accurately that I got a shower of snow and earth in my face while I was peering through the lookout-slit to take a bearing on the muzzle flash. We had to evacuate the O.P. and move back to the dugout. As soon as we got there the window was blown in and we had to nail up the gap.

The inevitable happened. Our line party was fired at from our wood, seventy yards to the rear of the dugout. Russian patrols had got behind us and cut the cable. Our men could see them. Later, our own patrols found that the Russians had trampled out a wide path in the wood behind the main fighting line, from which four telephone lines led to the rear. At noon on the 31st the Battery Commander came to the dugout. He made another attempt to occupy the observation post, together with Lieutenant Mack. It couldn't be done. The anti-tank gun fired immediately. They had a very close shave and were dazed for five minutes afterwards. It was a bad night. There were said to be three hundred men in P., ready to attack. If it had come off, they'd have got us. But we concentrated the fire of the whole regiment on the place, and a mighty bombardment it was. Afterwards we could hear the shrieks of the wounded.

Today we were relieved. On their way up, the reliefs were fired at and had to pull back. A sledge with equipment and baggage fell into the hands of the enemy. They made another attempt and this time they got through. At 12.30 we moved off, ten men and two sledges carrying a couple of wounded. We drove a Russian deserter before us (one of those who for the past two days have been roaming about the wood without food).

Five hundred yards from the O.P. we met an enemy patrol about fifteen strong. We ran straight into their flank. I saw the first one pressing himself under a fir tree on the left of the path. I beat him to it. When I got closer, I saw their advance party five yards away in a little dip; there were three of them and they tried to get away. My magazine was quickly empty. I jumped on them and managed to stop a couple, including the patrol leader. The third got away. I handed over the two prisoners to a comrade, reloaded, and went after the fugitive. I think I must have got him. In the meantime the patrol leader had tried to attack my companion with his pistol. My comrade would have shot him down, but his rifle jammed. The Russian's pistol wasn't cocked and my comrade smashed it out of his hand with his butt. Then they went for each other. I got back in time to join in. The rest of our party had gone on. They had opened fire on the main group of the patrol to the right of the path. I thought at the time we were going to deal with the whole lot, but suddenly we were alone. My comrade vanished too, and there I was with an infantryman with frost-bitten feet.

We had no losses. What with all the shouting and firing, the Russians had been so surprised by our attack, that they never managed to put up a systematic defence. The wounded cavalry lieutenant in charge of our party was pleased with his Gunners.

Now I mean to have a good sleep.

3rd of February, 1942. Promoted sergeant for "bravery in face of the enemy".

Our battery has fired more than a thousand rounds from its present position. It has repelled every enemy attack in our sector. The enemy would have to be totally inefficient not to discover our firing position—and the Russians aren't as inefficient as all that. Yesterday they sent over a reconnaissance plane and their third salvo got home. The carriage of No. 3 gun flew over the barrel, eighty rounds of ammunition went up, and a hit on the dugout caused nine casualties. One of the lads was lying three yards from the ammunition, but he didn't get an eyebrow singed, merely covered from head to foot with powder fouling.

Sergeant H., a fine, lively fellow belonging to our troop, was wounded at our O.P. during the night of the third. Early in the morning he and five other casualties were being evacuated on three sledges. On the sledge track the party met an enemy patrol. There were casualties among the escort, and later the wounded were found dead. The Pioneer officer, whom I've mentioned before, arrived here the same night shot through the arm. He had fought his way through the enemy with our Battery Commander. Of his remaining fifteen men he had only found two. No more prisoners are being taken in the front line.

The story of O.P. Red ended with our re-taking the main fighting line. The Russians cut off in the wood to the south-west can now await their certain end. However, O.P. Red had one more tough night of it. On the evening of February the 1st it was attacked from the wood behind by eighty to a hundred men. Lieutenant von Hindenburg was at the machine-gun, and officers and men were firing from behind a wooden stockade. At the same time Lieutenant Kroll pulled back the fire of our battery till it lay only thirty yards from the O.P. dugout. Two more attacks on the following nights are scarcely worth mentioning after that. The enemy's striking power is failing.

During the day we destroyed some smaller groups. Now the infantry are moving back into their dugouts again, after nine days and nights of huddling round tiny fires beneath shelters of fir branches, sleeping silent and numbed in the snow, unable to respond, as if they were drugged. The O.P. is to be abandoned.

Honour to your memory, O.P. Red! Everything around you is a shambles, heavy rafters smashed to matchwood; splintered tree stumps, broken equipment, dead horses, and many poor frozen bundles. Black is the snow before your red doorsteps. And yet you still stand. Your sheltering cave was everybody's refuge. You have become a symbol—O.P. Red!

There were five divisions against our one, we reached the limit of human endurance. And yet I saw moving instances of valour and courage. There was a staff-sergeant who in all those days stood like a rock in no-man's-land: he never once left his post, never once let his machine-gun jam, but roared at his men to stand their ground. There was a red-bearded sergeant, who didn't make a sound when they dressed his wounds, who laughed and called out cheerfully, as two comrades held him up: "I'll soon be back, sir!" And then there was a tall company commander who would edge himself slowly above the parapet, take aim carefully and fire, saying: "Round away," just as if he were on a rifle range. Such men still exist, and they can be worth more than a whole company.

CHAPTER V

WINTER ON THE CENTRAL SECTOR

TODAY I went up to the line again. Red is only half an O.P. now. The battlefield looks bad. The track to our one-time telescope post winds through a field of craters. The post itself had a direct hit today. Our own dugout shows signs of the storm too. The surrounding trees have been much thinned out: everything looks as if it had been plucked. There's no clean snow to be seen anywhere, it's a waste land. The steps down to the dugout are worn and covered with ice. Most of the time you slide down feet first and thunder against the door. But even if our hole is full of dirt and lice, even if the bricks fall out of the stove and the windows don't let in light any more, it's a safe place. Direct hits haven't hurt it, except for shaking a little dirt from the ceiling. Outside there'll be a rrrumph! But inside we feel fine and safe.

We're old friends now, the infantry and ourselves. We know each other by name and we get on fine. We share the same things, eating and drinking, the cold, the lice and the shelling. We're all in this together; we lay our sights on the same enemy. I'm sitting close to the window and it's difficult to write. It's in the middle of the night, 2 a.m. Most of us are asleep. But as the plank bed can't hold everybody, there are always some who sit up. Anyway, we can't all afford to sleep. Night and day, they are both much the same. You eat, you sleep at any old time and you don't know for how long, and you follow your trade. That's all it is, a trade—with moments of grim pleasure.

Yesterday some of the blankets which have been collected at home arrived. "How touching," we said, "how they smell of moth-balls, how clean!" You could see the parlour with the sofa, or the child's bed, or perhaps the young girl's room from which they came. We held them in our hands for a moment, smiling. How far away it all seemed, it could have been on another planet.

But don't worry, it's not as bad as all that. We'll find our way home again.

The sun has been shining day after day with the same radiance and in the entrance of our house, which is sheltered from the wind, it has licked a little of the snow away and left a moist patch. It's already a foretaste of spring.

The gifts were so generous that we've been able to pass on quite a lot of wool and fur clothing to our friends in the infantry. If our horses get through we'll have made it. The horses are one of our biggest problems. The truth is, the internal combustion engine is a dead loss in this winter warfare. Everything has to go by sledge. Where all the sledges come from is a mystery. But how all the horses survive is a greater one still. Hay has to come a three days' journey. The native ponies live by water and straw and beating. You'd hardly believe it. A stack of straw is a fantastic thing: it gets requisitioned, guarded, pinched at night; the repercussions reach Division, or even Corps. But six thousand horses finish it up in a few days.

We live on a queer star; it hits you whenever somebody arrives from reserve. Today a little man snowed in fresh from home. There he was in his new togs, clean and free from lice, dignified and full of innocent notions. We old trench rats sat round him enjoying the rabbit's company. It's funny, a man like that; touching in a way. Compared with him we're a rough, foul-mouthed lot of heathens. But how much healthier we are—sturdy enough to stand anything. The worst is probably over, but when he's sent up to the O.P., he may still see something.

As for the infantry replacements who came up today. . . . Gabel, our ration driver, met them staring open-eyed as they saw their first flares rising over the silent snowscape. Gabel is a dare-devil who every night races his horses up to the O.P. standing on his sledge with hand-grenades in his pockets. He described it wonderfully in his usual dry way.

The newcomers will have some surprises, but they'll have good teachers too. And so it will work out all right.

I am still rather weary, but for two days now I've been without a temperature. I keep blinking at the sun like a cat at the light. The sun is magnificent. When it rises in the morning mist, the snow is so glitteringly bright and the air so full of strong light that you have to turn away blinded.

Everything runs to extremes in this country. Would it ever be possible to get used to it? Time and again we try to accustom ourselves to the thought. Night after night we have lively discussions, trying to keep our brains active and our minds free from illusions.

We go on hoping we'll be relieved one day. We say so to each other and try to convince ourselves; but we're knocking at open doors, because we all want the same thing. It's only wishful thinking when we say: What, we do another offensive? With these horses? With this equipment? With this infantry? Can't you see the division is finished? The Russians will die of laughing when we come!

"The division's stretched over a front of twenty kilometres," someone said jokingly the other day. "It's like a small-town repertory company doing a procession. They march across the stage with solemn faces and race round the back to catch up again." Then there's another joke. "When the Colonel wanted to inspect the horses the other day somebody suggested putting out two cows on the left wing to make them look more."

21st of February, 1942. A drive in thick hoar frost to the O.P. We have got to relieve them in day-time, because Staff-Sergeant Schaper is getting his Iron Cross (First Class). The sun is shining, the snow-crystals blow off the trees like glass dust. The shaggy pony in his fire-red winter coat is trotting before the light sledge. We stretch ourselves luxuriously, blink at the glittering splendour and enjoy the drive.

The Russians are said to have set up an anti-tank gun over in P. I spun the wheel of the telescope and strained the eyes out of my head, but I couldn't discover anything. I was tempted. I was alone in the O.P. and I could be doing a little gunnery practice on my own.

In the afternoon I went to the forward infantry position where the observation was said to have been made. Wearing my new snow suit with snow-white trousers and jacket, I strolled along the trail through the wood and across a sunlit stretch of open ground to the "boot". The "boot" is a narrow cut in the ground, it runs towards the enemy and ends in a depression between ourselves and P. In it there's one dugout next to the other, the edge bristles with weapon pits, and the gully is wired.

Right at the edge of a spur was the machine-gun emplacement where I was going. I reported to Staff-Sergeant Uhl, who is holding the "boot" with his men. To tell the truth, the men are not much good, but a man like Uhl is worth a hundred.

I sat in his dugout for a while. How he's got them in hand! You can tell the superior confidence of an intrepid old soldier from every word he speaks. Uhl hasn't gone soft like so many others, he isn't chummy in the way which is only a sign of weakness, and his men respect him. In his burrow of a dugout all the weapons lie neatly stacked, the rifles in a row, the hand-grenades lined up ready for use. On one shelf there are books and writing material, and on another a smartly dressed row of mess tins. You may laugh about it, but now I know that things like that are more than mere show—they're a sign of good soldiering. Just ask an ordinary soldier if he'd rather have a superior like that or some other kind. You get your answer without hesitation: give me the Staff-Sergeant any day!

The ordinary soldier knows well enough that at the decisive

moment his life depends on the courage and ability of his leader. He has learned it from experience.

I was guided forward through the "boot" and I climbed the rise to the advance post. There was only a wall of snow to give cover from sight. Four hundred yards away you could see the enemy's machine-gun nests and snipers' foxholes. But I couldn't see the anti-tank gun. A pity.

Lately I have found it difficult to concentrate. I'm very tired— tired and worn out. I feel quite empty. I don't feel like writing. A letter home is a terrible strain. The difference between what I write and what I feel is too great. Music from the wireless doesn't interest me any more; it gives me no pleasure, no relaxation. When I read things which once would have interested me enormously, like the latest French political writing, my thoughts wander off.

Is there any point in it? If I come back from this war, I'll be sick: sick in everything that only love can heal. The 427th Regiment[1] has come back from the battle of Rzhev with 280 men. That's scarcely the strength of a battalion.

10th of March, 1942. In the past few days they've collected the Russians who fell in the fighting at the end of January and in early February. It's not out of piety, but for the sake of hygiene. The heaps are considerable. The "boot" alone yielded more than sixty, the victims of our battery. I walked between the piles of bodies to discover my reactions. I had no sense of gruesomeness nor of disgust, I was entirely without strong emotions of any kind. The mangled bodies are thrown on the heaps, frozen stiff and in the oddest attitudes. Finis. They're done with, they'll be burnt. But first, they are stripped of clothing by Russians—old men and children. It's horrible. Seeing it, one sees an aspect of the Russian mentality which one simply can't understand. They smoke and make jokes; they grin. You can't believe that anyone could be so unfeeling.

[1] *Translator's note*: equivalent to a British brigade.

The sledges with the bodies are driven by ten to twelve-year-old children. Some of the corpses have half a head missing, others are in shreds. They lie twisted one on top of another, frozen green and brown, in their poor nakedness. Only now does one realise, very slowly, what this people can endure and of what it is capable.

The sky was hanging low and grey over the wide countryside; the wind was singing in the trees, catching up the snow and driving it in thin streamers over the hills. But in the wood it was quiet, and the little fir-tits and linnets seemed to belong to a different world. Ivan dropped leaflets in which he paid a special compliment to our division. He calls us the bloodhounds and incendiaries of Kalinin and assures us that none of us will ever see our homes again.

We derive a certain grim pleasure from it. Let him come. Tonight we've all been put on the alert, but up to now it has been as quiet as usual. Perhaps the machine-guns have been a little more nervous. . . . Our friend from the infantry is lying with his head on the table. I am all alone.

Radiant blue skies alternate with grey-shrouded days. But one thing is always the same: the quietness on our sector. Yesterday at dawn one of our anti-tank guns scored a couple of lightning hits on two of the Russian machine-gun nests. It was over before they knew where they were. But apart from that there's been nothing doing. From time to time I race without coat or gloves to the telescope, only to find that there's no sign of life on Ivan's side. He must be concentrating his forces on another sector. Over on the left there was some pretty heavy rumbling this morning.

We sit by the fire picking breadcrumbs out of the remaining tea. There's some snow melting in a mess tin and a slice of bread toasting on the stove. We hang our hands between our knees without talking.

We're often silent here, because everything that can be said has been said. The vastness of the country throws you back on yourself, and at times when nothing much is happening your thoughts begin to stray. We've come a long way since the weeks when we were devoured by everything that happened. Now our view of things is more mature, and we see them in better perspective.

One thing seems to be true of nearly everybody: soldiers in the East acquire a deeper insight into the purity and imperishable worth of the bonds of affection. They become deeply conscious of how much they cling to their wives and children, till their sadness becomes like a dedication, and under a cloak of rough words their feeling grows into something sacrosanct. They learn to be reverent again.

Outside there is a snowstorm, and our "house" becomes more of an island than ever. I'm back from the O.P. One night was quite enough up there. To even things up, the field post office has done me proud with letters and cigarettes, biscuits, sweets, nuts, and a pair of wrist muffs. It touched me very much as I put them on. I thought of all the loving care, all the little sacrifices behind the gifts. I can well imagine what it meant. I am grateful.

A little *entr'acte*: the Battery Commander showing a new officer round—"By the way, down there on the gun-sites you'll find a number of sergeants who aren't one hundred per cent soldiers, but they're decent enough fellows. Some gunners, too; Eastern fronters, but very useful. Don't upset them; don't try to chivvy them, it's no good. I tried myself at first, but I've come to the conclusion that things are better as they are. This isn't the time for it."—This incident is a good illustration. The Old Man is quite right.

To go back to the letters from home. It's very moving to feel all the anxiety and love which goes out to us; it makes us happy, and yet it shows only too painfully under what tension we are all living. How many fervent thoughts and wishes extend to this front every hour; what a bridge they make across the vast distance. The power of all this love, the devotion of mothers, makes all the big phrases seem miserable and pale.

What are words compared with all this suffering? All the same, it may help to be honest. Though I may not tell you everything, I have never left out anything of importance apart from figures and place names, which as a soldier I must not mention. The figures are serious, I admit; and anyway, you write in your letters that all the trains with the wounded and the frost-bite cases tell an unmistakable story. It's true that our fate was hanging by a thread for a little while. When our infantry were in the open, the frost-bite cases were at their worst and day by day our numbers were dwindling. But the situation was never desperate. The attack of despondency lasted only for a paralysing fraction of a second, then our courage returned, and with it the certainty that we'd get by.

Also we have seen that the Russians aren't supermen either, and we've learnt a lot. We had to pay for our experience, it's true. To those who are left, the "old brigade", nothing much can happen now. It's only dangerous for the young replacements. They have had the greatest number of casualties. They don't have the experience, they don't know the signs, like noticing the tip of one's nose going white; they don't know how to look after themselves. Often they have to be sent back after a few days and when I see them in the line, harmless and unsuspecting in their childish innocence, I could cry.

So you need not worry too much about me. If a bullet gets you, there's no arguing. But you can avoid bullets, if you know how. And believe me, I've got a nose for flying metal. Other risks don't concern me anyway, or at least all those connected with the cold. And that danger gets less from day to day. Courage and vitality are returning. Slowly we're getting back our initiative and confidence.

I've had another night out in the new O.P. There was a pretty strong snowstorm, which blew drifts over our approach track and the communication trench. I cleared the trench three times with a shovel, but in the morning we were snowed up again. Otherwise it was quite snug. We extended the stove-pipe into the trench; after that the stove drew fantastically, the pipe got red-hot, and the mess tins of snow started hissing the moment they were put on the hot-plate. When I've said this, I've said all; warmth is everything.

During the day we shovelled the track clear; it was fairly hard work, the sun was shining and I was soon working in my shirt-sleeves. But tonight there's another storm, the snow pricks you like fine needles, and tomorrow we shall probably find that all our work was for nothing. There are people who get mad over things like that. But I've made up my mind not to care any more. My muscles are tired, I've been pummelled by the wind and sun, and I like it. Happy? Yes, and why not?

Yesterday there was a snowstorm from the north-east which beat all previous ones. Visibility was four hundred yards. At the O.P. you couldn't see a thing.

In the early hours of the morning the enemy tried to attack R. again. R. is on a height, beyond the river Desna, which is the real boundary between us. But as one can see into our whole main fighting line from there, we are holding on to the place. We put down four barrages in a semi-circle round it, the whole regiment together. Whenever the enemy attacked, every gun roared out. The indescribable weather made it necessary to push forward another observer to watch the right flank of R.

The headwind was so strong that despite a special calculation beyond the map distance, one battery fired three hundred yards short; but these conditions are exceptional. I was with Budde, who may not be a "soldier" but was just the right man for such a job. For three and a half hours we ski-ed diagonally to the wind, up to our ankles in loose snow and blinded by snow crystals. Our cap comforters were frozen stiff and at one stage I was worried about my finger-tips. But we got there, even though it meant crossing a stretch of flat country at the end. At the company they were pleased to get extra help. We went with the forward observer of a light battery who had been up there for some time. The house next door was the observation post of a mortar troop, with living quarters nicely arranged in the stable. Even the parlour was well preserved, apart from a hole in the ceiling through which snow-water was dripping. These two houses were the last ones habitable, though both had had their chimneys shot away. Visibility was so bad that we could make a fire without hesitation. It was very snug.

So long as there's a fire life is all right. We had a telephone cable connecting the mortars, the company, the battalion and our own O.P. From there a line went through our own exchange to the gun-sites and the computing section. There wasn't much to do. I stood in the damaged attic where I could watch the guns ranging on a target. The target could only be guessed at, but once again, in spite of the morning's experience, the rounds were falling three hundred yards too short. The wind had grown even stronger. Afterwards when I combed my hair I found my hand full of snow.

The night was quiet. The Russians tried to attack R. but got stuck in the snow after two hundred yards. Simultaneously they did a surprise shoot on our village. As a rule, they have given up this kind of thing because they always get flanking fire in return. Two shells fell in front of our stable, another one hit it.

The infantry crept from their quarters, afraid that the wretched structure might go up in flames. They came into our room at two in the morning. Budde woke up and heard them saying: "Look how these gunners go on sleeping, the thick-skinned bastards!" He told me about it on our way home. We were called back at nine in the morning.

We covered the entrance to the dugout with branches so that the inmates won't get snowed under again. But now it's developing into an ice grotto, because the snow is melted by the stove-pipe and the warm air which comes up. The communication trench was filled in long ago. When you miss the invisible trail you break into the snow up to the waist; then you have to jerk yourself on to your back or stomach and roll about to get your legs free; finally you go on by rolling and crawling. That way you reach the snow parapet, where you dive straight into the dugout like a fox down his hole.

It's fantastic, this snow burrow. From below, you can just see the opening with the snow whirling round it, glistening in the sun. The light breaks in like a broken, roaring waterfall, growing stronger from day to day.

I took the binoculars and leaned across the snow-wall. The wind blew straight into my face, and as I was standing there I thought: it won't take long till I'm completely powdered over with snow. It settled in little mounds on my gloves, nestled in every crease of my snow-shirt, and piled up in the hood. It was pleasant to watch two line-men patrolling with the wind blowing their coats round their legs, to see the snow whirling and bounding round the Russian dugouts. A few lost Ivans appeared and vanished in the mad dance, bent down, searched for something, ran to and fro. They were obviously working so much harder than I, who could glide back at any time into the shelter of my hole, watch the snow melt on my boots and my white trousers start steaming, and enjoy the smell of toasted bread rising pleasantly to my nose.

When I woke up my companions it was half-past five. The stove threw out all its heat once more, but then it had to be put out, because on a clear day the smoke can be seen for miles. A clear day it turned out to be, a day with the bluest of skies, sparkling and shining with blinding glory. Against the pale blue there was a delicate rainbow caused by ice crystals which the wind had carried to higher regions. The sun was so warm that I stretched out in the snow for a sun-bathe.

We dug a new trench to the wood. It was six feet deep. When my companion threw the snow high over the side, it gave a golden flash and purled sparkling in the breeze. I was worried in case the

THE OUTERMOST FRONTIER

Russians could see it. Visibility was wonderful. I looked over the
terrain with the binoculars and made out whole systems of field
fortifications which I had missed before. Then we took turns with
the digging, working with our faces to the sun until evening.
Now my face is burning and the skin is tight over my cheek-
bones. How I enjoy the warm water in the evening, and fresh
underwear, and the cream on my face and hands. What a pleasure
it was to get my mail. There was quite a lot, and it didn't take
long to get here. Letters posted on 27th of February. It's wonderful, at last one has the feeling of really being in touch.

In the meantime the dugout has become even more handsome.
In a poplar-wood frame the miniatures of the Manesse Codex[1]
shine out in red and gold like Russian ikons. There is a field
letter-box, and a bookshelf and newspaper-rack are arriving
tomorrow. Slowly everything is being given a place and we feel
at home. It's a pleasant crew, a small circle of rather select people
as is often the case in an O.P. We talk in the evenings about art
and literature, history, languages and philosophy, or sometimes
we recite forgotten poetry and dream of the past and the future.
Our ages are very different; two of us about thirty and two about
twenty. The lieutenant is in the middle—he's twenty-four.
Different generations, you might think. But no, that's the surprising thing. We share the same ideas, the same imaginings and
wishes, the same doubts and the same ambitions.

But perhaps it isn't so surprising, because here it's the true values
which are in the balance. High-sounding phrases don't ring true,
a man becomes his true self. Will some inner force grow out of all
this, a serious gathering of forces, a turning towards the inner
Realm? Will these forces be acknowledged, and will they once
again determine the standards and values of our lives? That's a
question which the future will decide. Today we are faced with
other problems which we have to solve without stopping to
weigh them.

[1] The thirteenth-century illuminated manuscript at Heidelberg.

64

Today I've been firing. It was to have been a little gunnery practice, strictly according to regulations, on what seemed to me a totally uninteresting enemy position. I kept up a quiet grumble, throwing out hints that target-point 316 would be a much better proposition, that I had set my heart on it and would enjoy firing on it much more. But they said no, it was too difficult; there was a wood behind it and shots which went beyond the target would disappear; also there was dead ground, and in any case . . . I felt very bitter. But then the observers came through with the message: "Enemy entrenching at point 316. They're jumping about in snow-shirts, and there's a new dugout already finished." Reports came in one after another. Fate was favouring my design. So in the end I did fire on point 316. Hooray! I made them dive for it, it was as good as a holiday.

Since yesterday it has shown signs of thawing, and although the big thaw is only expected in two weeks, our problems are increasing and preparations for the mud period are being speeded up. For example, in front of our village are some fifty horses which fell victim to the winter. Although the civilian population has contributed assiduously to getting rid of them, the carcasses have still to be disposed of. The most practical way is to burn them. It takes a lot of wood and we can't actually achieve crematorium-heat. However, it's a proved and effective method. There will be some dead Russians too when the snow has disappeared.

No, our trade isn't elegant. But that's the way it is. We've had acknowledgement that we did a good job in the past few weeks. The Battery Commander and Lieutenant von Hindenburg have been mentioned in despatches. Von Hindenburg has been promoted Captain. One of the battalion commanders has the Gold German Cross, and the regimental commander, Colonel Danhauser, has the Knight's Cross.

Outside, a storm is sweeping the country, whipping up the snow. It's like fine smoke, wrapping up everything, so that only the tree-tops are visible and the villages are swimming like dis-embodied islands. The Russians are quite right, the thaw will come in a fortnight. But what do I care. When the storm gets me by the neck I turn up my collar, and when I lift my eyes I see through all this witch's cauldron a tiny patch of blue, which tells me that the force of the winter is broken, that it's only behaving so angrily today because spring is already at its heels.

At 1815 a message came that Staff-Sergeant Schaper had been killed. Shot through the head. Finished. *Le chevalier sans peur et sans reproche.*

On March the 29th I took over the place which had so suddenly become vacant at O.P. Red—O.P. Red, where I know every inch and cranny. I took over the equipment of the man who had been my teacher, and I took over his job.

When I look at the equipment and Schaper's careful and con-scientious notes, I don't want to talk about my feelings. It's war, and we are soldiers. I will only say a few words about this man, whose protection spelt safety for the infantry, whose name was known far beyond the battery, and whom I knew since the day I joined the unit in France.

He was quiet and modest and so self-effacing, open and without pretension that he could easily have been overlooked. We jokingly called him "the lion of Bellavino and Litino", yet we did so with sincerity and secret admiration. He would laugh and be deprecating. "Children, don't be silly!" he would say. But in fact he was out in front in every difficult situation, always at the most dangerous spots, everywhere there was something going on. He could do a shoot, as can only few, with a rare talent for mastering the whole theory. He knew his trade inside out. Up-right and blameless; that was Herbert Schaper, who fell on a perfectly quiet day, the victim of a single bullet. The driver who brought him back was overcome with tears.

People say—how often I have heard it in these last few days—"It was fate," or "It was pre-ordained." But is it true? Isn't it just a pathetic attempt to discover some sense in what happens, because we are too cowardly to face the senselessness of it? Is it that our weak minds need a crutch? Alas, we won't get away with it so cheaply.

What happens makes no sense and follows no human law. War strikes blindly, and if it knows a law, then that law is to strike down the best. "Those who spare themselves are spared," says Borée. He's right. Those who do not spare themselves are exposed. They look out for themselves as best they can. Their will to live tries to defeat the law, and the more clearly they understand the law, the quicker and stronger they become.

For here you cannot resign yourself; nobody accepts his fate. We're no lambs of God; we defend ourselves. Even though the fist of war may sometimes grab us so tightly that we have to say "God help us", the faith which buoys us up is the faith in our own strength and its secret sources. We trust not in God but in the calm care with which we perform our necessary tasks.

We are exposed so long as the course of events is beyond our control. It can't be avoided. We adapt ourselves, trying to keep lively and alert. That way you can reduce the danger. But you can't eliminate it. The bullet you hear has already passed you, and you couldn't have known which way it was flying. That's the sort of situation we've had to accept—but we haven't resigned ourselves to it. There's a vital difference.

Yesterday the Russians managed it at last. At least, they got as far as our wire, which is only twenty-five yards from the snow wall. "I got there dead at the right moment," said Gabel, the ration driver, "—just in time to baptise my Schmeiser. I jumped up next to the sergeant and let them have it. Off they went through the hole in the wire, and when I looked, there wasn't a perisher left."

Tonight the gun crews were called out eleven times. The telephone kept buzzing all night. The Battery Commander's voice sounded a bit hoarse, and I wasn't too happy either. I've been witnessing this commotion round my old O.P. from the gun position, but even here you feel sore at being dragged from your sleep all the time. Yesterday afternoon the Russians were firing at a stretch of ground between the gun position and the village. Nice big Mediums; we had a grand-stand view. We stood outside, hands in our pockets, looking at it all with a specialist's eye. It was very funny to see how people ran along the road—an amusing game for the spectators, but not so funny for the participants. However, they can laugh about it afterwards. Danger overcome increases one's zest for life; and some of us actually seek it. Playing with death has a great attraction. The smell of battle makes you want to be there.

If you know a particular sector as well as I know O.P. Red, you feel it's the place where you should be. It's "your" sector they're fighting over. As every message comes in, I know that "this" is here and "that" is there. I can visualise the country, the folds in the ground, the "pillbox", the snow wall, and the snow dugout from which my comrades are being fired at. In short, I belong there; when I go outside and hear the firing there thickening up, I feel personally involved.

At nightfall someone was playing a mouth-organ; folk songs, *heimat lieder*. We felt quite changed. Dangerous stuff—it makes people home-sick.

We went outside the house to listen to the great war-song which the shells make when, with eight charges, they leave the muzzles in a brilliant flash and swell into a glorious diapason. We watched the fall of the Russian shells which were dropping sparsely into the field. We only once interrupted our game of chess today, when a small hit broke our windows. We crept into the dugout for a little while, thinking that perhaps it was wiser. . . . But after that once, we didn't repeat the performance.

Please don't write of your hopes that we'll be relieved, and don't call the job we have done "superhuman".

There is no question of relief: we're staying here to the end and sticking it out. Besides, men don't achieve the superhuman. We have achieved something, yes; but we hate public praise. It's embarrassing and leaves a bad taste. Hero-worship is a dubious thing. Exaggerations give us pains in the stomach. One shouldn't praise anybody to the skies before he's dead. Then, if he's killed, one should write: "He fell for Germany." Nothing more. Whether he gave his life willingly, and what he felt in doing it, that's his concern. Generally it was different.

There's something we talk about again and again. It's as old as the world, thought about and talked about a thousand times, and yet it becomes more and more important to us. I'm not talking about myself here, it's not a personal question. It's a question which in some form or other occupies everybody out here. "What happens when I die? Wouldn't it be a good thing if I were to live on through a child?" Some people say "No, you have no right to leave a widow with a small child. . . ."

But it seems to me that their argument isn't very strong.

The more a man is exposed to the loneliness here, to the enforced chastity and the thought that the body is a frail vessel, the stronger becomes the urge to see his blood reborn. It's nature crying for her rights—it's as if they still owed her a tribute.

It's not the reaction against years of abstinence which accounts for the increase in births and marriages after a bloody war, but this urge to live on in one's children. These men feel that their life has not been fulfilled. All their petty reasoning has faded in the face of ultimate forces, the almightiness of nature and the cry of their blood that wants to live on and refuses to be extinguished until it has been transmitted to another generation.

The war is far from being over. "I want to have a child," the men say, "soon, on my next leave."

CHAPTER VI

THE STRANGE LIFE OF THE FRONT

ON April the 17th, 1942,[1] I went out in the afternoon to gather some catkins and budding twigs. But afterwards the bunch lay unnoticed on the table: Sergeant Godowski had been killed. So once again I found myself taking over from someone for the last time. That was the day before yesterday. However, I didn't go up to the post in the end; we have shifted the look-out several hundred yards to the right and now I'm sitting on a swaying platform in the branches of a fir tree. It's on the edge of the "boot", with a good dugout close by. The way up is well covered; it goes through the gully, where the sunshine is already quite strong. The snow-water roars in a torrent towards the Dersha, and the chaffinches and tits are acting as if it were summer.

Yesterday I saw the first brimstone butterfly; at midday I sat with the infantry boys on a tree trunk in the gully and stretched myself out in the sun. But in the morning the ground is still frozen hard and one can walk with ease over the last of the snowfields. At least, when I went out this morning at five o'clock I didn't get my feet wet. That's equally as pleasant as the sunshine and the butterfly, not to mention the ants, which one now finds in one's trousers instead of the lice.

Now they have gone, all my old friends of Six Company. Sergeant Wissig, the tireless company headquarters sergeant; Weisske, the medical orderly; Froehlich, the telephonist; Sergeant Roth, the friend with whom I sat in the sun; Heintze, the young staff-sergeant; and finally, the irrepressible August. How many wonderful (and how many awful) hours we spent together!

[1] On this day Helmut Pabst made his last will.

What a farewell party! We had quite a large unofficial hoard of ammunition, some light and heavy mortars and a number of surplus machine-guns. So on the night of the 19th we had a farewell shoot which was great fun. The Russians had already been cowed during the day by our artillery: forty-two rounds on L., forty-nine on D., sixty on Sh., and forty on the area round N.

There was such a roaring and rolling along the front that up on our platform in the tree we were hopping from one leg to another. Towards evening, August did a "surprise shoot" on P. with his mortar, a private little fireworks display of fifty rounds. After that my own mortar contributed a show every hour. At the stroke of midnight the machine-guns started up and the whole front got rebellious. Telephones started ringing: "What's going on up there? Is Ivan attacking?"—"Oh, no," we replied, "a farewell shoot. . . ." We were splitting our sides with laughter.

The new crowd arrived in the evening, Pioneers. Who was the first person to come towards me but Sergeant Jansen, an old acquaintance from Daoulas. With his machine-gun section he took over the dugout by my look-out in the tree. The next person I met in the company headquarters was Ferdi Keip from Frankfurt, with whom I share a thousand memories from the days of the Youth Movement. Ferdi and I moved with our men into one dugout. About midnight a biggish lump of clay fell on his stomach, so in the morning we started to revet the wells. August gave me a Russian machine pistol as a farewell present; it was an enormous thing, seventy-two rounds per drum, American pattern. We collected ammunition for it from the wood, where all we wanted was simply lying about.

Another company has arrived on my sector, sixty-eight men strong. In the last few days I've had nothing to do but show the infantry round, explain the ground to the C.O. and the company commanders, point out our barrage zone, and range the new mortars. We have brought up a roving gun, which with six charges and a following wind just manages to reach Sh. Ivan is getting a bit cheeky because of the inexperience of the new crowd, but we'll soon have him under control again.

Our Russian Vassil has done well with the battery. We picked him up with thirteen comrades in Kalinin. They had been left behind in a prison camp and didn't want anything more to do with the Red Army. We took them all with us, and they helped us to bring many a horse through the winter. But Vassil was especially active and attached to us. For that he's been given a special testimonial from the battery and is being sent off with rations on the road to Berlin. He used to be a tractor driver; now he'll help to build tanks. But Vassil says he doesn't really want to go to Germany, he wants to stay with the battery.

When I strolled up to the look-out at half-past four this morning, the wood was white again and the trees had vanished in a veil of falling snow. But by ten the bog was already steaming in the sun, and as I passed under the dripping boughs I was sprinkled with glistening beads of water.

The nights are growing restless. Shelling is becoming more frequent. Mortars and field and anti-tank guns shower us with dirt, noise and splinters. In between, the night is laced by machine-guns and the swift network of tracer. Prelude to the May Day.

Yesterday we could already hear them singing over in their dugouts in P. Gramophone records were blaring and the wind carried threads of propaganda speeches. Comrade Stalin has issued vodka, long live comrade Stalin! Long live the Red Army! Our own men are standing soberly at their posts.

At 2300 hours I went to sleep. At 0030 hours I went up to the O.P. again. The telephone kept waking me. The night was clear with moonlight. Bursts of machine-gun fire were spreading through the wood and rifle grenades were exploding with sharp cracks. The frost on the grass crackled under my feet. In puddles and ruts on the boggy path there was the gleam of ice.

The enemy was attacking on the sector to the left, trying to cut off our bridgehead beyond the little river. The telephone gave a double buzz. The look-out. The line began to get lively; hurried conversations, reports and enquiries. Fire control. Behind us the guns started firing, the shells sped in quick succession, tearing a sharp curve through the night and ending in abrupt explosions. Then after a while it got quiet.

I went outside. Far on the right the artillery was grumbling. Some houses were burning in G. On the stretch of grass in front of our wire the few shrubs were indistinct in the pale moonlight. The man on guard by the machine-gun stood silent and motionless, as if he were part of the landscape.

But the silence was deceptive. Suddenly there was the sigh of the treacherous mortars once more, and the howl of high-velocity shells. The man at the machine-gun tore back the cocking handle and fired burst after burst. At the same time the Heavies were searching for our gun positions. One of our batteries replied. To the left, on the edge of a wood, an enemy patrol was being wiped out with grenades. If they feel like attacking, let them come, I thought. But they didn't want to. You could tell it from the pauses in the music. There was none of the crescendo which opens an attack, the thickening-up of fire which is meant to drive the enemy under cover and wear down his morale. We lay at the alert, but we knew they wouldn't come. We lay there watching the sky in the East turn red beneath the light turquoise of the night, changing into a delicate milky blue till at last the sun rose, like an enormous ball of fire over the hills. Now the brass flights of tracer are only passing intermittently to and fro, as if in a game.

I have set down the events of May the 1st during the night of May the 2nd. We are still on a special alert. I am sitting in the dugout and writing throughout the night. By my side, stuck into a hole in the revetting, is a piece of wood holding the candle. There are also two prints: "The Garden of Eden" by a Rhenish master, and "The Flight into Egypt" by Hans Baldung. Some people may have been surprised that my voice should always have sounded so fresh and lively whenever the telephone buzzed—and that was pretty often. "Going forward into the gully now to lay mines; watch out you don't fire!"—"Enemy patrol moving about on the left. We're going after them; we'll report as soon as we're back." So it went on all the time. However, at 6.15 in the morning I certainly grumbled. I had just slept for three-quarters of an hour when a call came: "Tanks advancing from east of P.— Have you spotted them?" Go to the devil with your tanks, I thought to myself, cursing. Into the phone I said: "Yes, sir," and lay down again; I didn't even pass on the message, because it was quite clear to me that it was only a gun tractor. And even if it had been a tank, what of it? Until it got to the gully, I could have done nothing about it, and when it came out on our side, it would have been too late anyhow. To hell with the "tank".

A tank! Just think of it! What would it want, alone in the wood? If a tank wanted to play catch with us, let it try. In cases like that, we've always got concentrated charges ready, not to mention the special mines. Let them come! When you're prepared for a danger it loses its threat. It's like that with all dangers. That's why I think the safest place is with the fighting troops. The front line is the soldier's own territory. There are no partisans there; no slinking civilian would dare come near it, he'd be shot at on sight. The rest is clear. I know what's waiting for me. I can act accordingly. There are tricks, but no underhand tricks. That makes the frontline the cleanest zone of all. Also in other respects.

The nights are cold. The earth is frozen again. Snow squalls wander through the changing light. But if you shoot with a pistol into a birch tree, the sap spurts out, and it drips from the branches where shell splinters have cut into the tree-tops. I believe in the birch tree.

When I read letters from home, it seems as if the people there find the thought of this summer and a second winter unbearable. It is not unbearable. One's soul will lose a little more of its power to soar. We shall become more serious and more hard, remoter from everything that's light. But against the grey background of our existence our dreams acquire a brightness they have never known before, the youth we have lost appears to us in a radiant beauty, outshining everything.

Our sister battery has pulled out and rolled off somewhere else. We have swung round our barrels. The O.P. and our left-flank look-out are now on the right, but my old observation post in front of P. remains. Old O.P. Red is holding out stubbornly; it seems to be the centre of everything. I have relieved one of No. 10 Battery's observers. We started out at two in the morning when there was already a strip of light in the East. There was just enough snow to silhouette men and horses. We rode in silence at a light trot, following the track, which, blurred by fresh snow, ran through the wood and over the hills towards the front. We met some of our troops riding on a little cart; they reached for their weapons but uncocked them with relief as we drew level.

It was half-light when we stopped at the first barns of N. I sent back the horses, the first bullets began to whistle, and we went on on foot. We passed through communication trenches, across cables and wreckage to the company command post.

N. lies rather low, on a bank of the river Dersha. It is easily overlooked from every side. The opposite bank, where the burnt-out remains of I. stand, is a little higher. On the left is P., which I know so well; now I have a clear view of the back and the other side of it. There's nothing much left of N., but there's a good view from the attic of one of the two remaining houses, and our dugout is nicely hidden in the ruins of the other.

The front continues its strange existence. There's rolling and banging and rattling, the shells sing through the air, ricocheting and exploding. The flares sail up, white and red, and for a moment the planks and duckboards stand out in the chalk-white fluttering light, allowing one to make a few quick steps and a jump. Then the night becomes darker still, and once more you grope through the wet, slippery trenches. The trenches continue left and right as far as you can imagine, and in the night you sometimes feel the whole extension of the immense front.

The dugout is seven foot wide and ten and a half long. It's not much for six men. There's the regular soldier, Staff-Sergeant von Hoven from Allenstein; Strauss, a proud father of twenty-one, from the Hegau; Pfeil, the tall baby-faced schoolboy from Marburg; Lizon, the greedy Silesian; Onischke, a corporal from Koenigsberg; and myself, the lawyer from Frankfurt. We are in two lots of three, the advanced observers of a howitzer battery, and some heavy infantry guns. As long as one lot lie in their bunks the others have room. You might think that under these circumstances there would be some danger of bickering or even a proper row. But on the contrary, the dugout is governed by general goodwill, friendly tolerance and unquenchable good humour, all of which inject a ray of cheerfulness into the most unpleasant situation. If somebody wants to wash in the tiny space between the stove and the door we move the table between the bunks, and one person can still just sit there. The others stay in their bunks. When three of us are eating, the rest sit on the beds of planks and watch them. We have called the dugout the "U-boat", because it's just as neat as one. It doesn't work just anyhow: it works *well*—because there's always a joke, and we're always ready for a laugh. It works because the East Prussians, the Hessians, the Silesian and the *Aleman* are all good fellows. They all belong to the same family and are sustained by the will to make life easy. We share a common life, not so much in danger (of which we scarcely speak seriously) but in the more human things. These latter appear in the evening, when Strauss shows round the picture of his baby, and Onischke the picture of his wife. The others know that these objects are sacred and untouchable. No matter how coarse a man is, here he becomes quiet and serious. Perhaps it's because in everybody's mind there's the picture of a woman and a home, and thinking of that home which he left long ago and to which he longs to return on some distant, un-imaginable day, he falls silent. . . .

In the first light of dawn today we struck at a machine-gun post which had been enfilading the whole valley. While the shells of a heavy infantry gun and three heavy mortars were plastering the post, the tracer of our machine-gun poured straight into the embrasures of other enemy positions. At the second shell-burst a flare went up over the way; into the third swayed the figure of a man. The whole thing lasted only a few minutes, a neat piece of co-operation. Afterwards everything was quiet for a while. So quiet that you could hear lumps of earth plopping into the river.

From five o'clock until nine I slept. Then the three of us moved into a new dugout which had been vacated by the advance look-out of No. 11 Battery. We cleaned it up, made ourselves at home and pottered about in the trench. In the afternoon I did a little ranging. Now it's 2200 and night has fallen. My two men went to collect our rations. I'll be glad when they're back: about this time the enemy starts his traversing fire.

During the night I went with Lizon to fetch water. There's only one well. By daytime you can't get near it and even at night Ivan gives it his special attention. At the first try my bucket fell in. There was a little jerk and a splash, and gone was a valuable piece of equipment. At the second attempt the rope got entangled in the windlass. That was bad; we had to do something about it or the others would have had no water that night. Lizon was hanging half inside the shaft, swearing like a bargee. He knocked over our child's bath, water and all. Every time a flare went up we froze. But finally it was done. When we were back in the trench Lizon gave a deep sigh. We looked at the watch: we had been away an hour and a half.

It's a mild evening and the rainy wind blends with the green of the countryside. Russian children have nailed up a pole between two trees and tied a rope to it. They have been swinging all afternoon. Their cries and laughter fill the village street. They're barefoot, dressed in rags, covered in mud; but they're happy and healthy. Towards evening one of our lads may join in the game and help Vanya or Tania to swing even higher. Our men are sitting on the doorsteps playing mouth-organs and singing into the night: "In the dugouts, on the rocks . . . " Later you'll only see a cigarette glowing here or there in the dark.

Martin, the ethnologist, who's now an infantry lieutenant, has told me in a letter that it gives him a great deal of pleasure to be ruling seven villages, trying to get the agriculture going again. He says he'd enjoy it even more if he weren't sure to be sent off again on another job.

It's true we have hated this country and fought against it; it has brought us suffering and home-sickness. But it's beautiful too—full of joys and undiscovered treasures.

The O.P. is situated by the railway line. The dugout is built into the side of the embankment, weather-beaten and heavy as an alpine hut and big as a dance hall. It's a strange building. I climbed the embankment and walked up to the look-out along the wooded path. There's bog, luxuriant wilderness, and a pool of warm brown water where myriads of mosquitoes are breeding in the sunlight. There are some gleaming alders we have thrown into the pool to make a little causeway. Then there's a vast ant-hill and a couple of shell craters before you come to the tree platform which swings groaning in the wind. The little hut hangs hidden among the tops of three fir trees; you let yourself be rocked and listen to the cuckoo. The fir trees already have tiny blood-red cones, which glow amid the green.

CHAPTER VII

THE END OF THE FIRST YEAR

*In the early summer of 1942, the main German effort was on the front
of Army Group South, where Hitler's quest for oil dictated a new drive
towards Maikop and the Caucasus. Following an abortive Russian
attack towards Kharkov, the German offensive was launched on June
28th, when the 4th Panzer Army (now transferred) broke into the
country between the Don and the Donetz, followed by von Paulus'
6th Army, whose task was to capture Stalingrad and secure the left
flank. All this left the Central Sector in comparative quiet.*

NOTHING much is happening. In the South the offensive
rolls on. Here we have still a breathing space. Slowly, bit
by bit, we're putting off our numbness like a tight suit.
Now we realise how blind and unfeeling the winter made us.

It's more than one would like to admit. I walked through the
hollow back to the O.P., letting the young branches run through
my hands and standing for a while in a clearing. A cloud-bank
stretched from the north across the pale evening sky. How vast
is the sky over Russia!

Day after day machine-gun bursts whistle over our cover. At
night the wood echoes with their whipping. Nothing happens: then
somebody gets up and goes outside the dugout, and a few seconds
later he's dead. The night was quiet; it was only a single burst, but
it got him. You say: "Damn it, he was a good lad," and next day
you see the wreath the boys have made, with bunches of red fir
cones, like the blossoming of a wound. You see his face again, just
as it was when he went outside. Then it gets blurred.

We have had a Sergeant Braun in our sector for a short time
and he's going away today. He was in charge of the machine-gun

section near my look-out post. He would stay awake while I was asleep. Our reports would complement each other. At night I would send him music which I got from somewhere on the lines, and neither of us drank his schnapps by himself. He was the specialist who set the dugouts in P. on fire and burnt down the last barns. In stony calm he fired round after round of tracer, leaning against a tree, sights at 600. Round after round at the same spot till it started to smoke. Yesterday he said: "What, volunteer for a patrol? Not me. I've had enough." But today he cursed because he hadn't been there. In the night they found that the firing positions in the Russian trench were empty. They passed by the dugouts and were talked to by the Russian sentry in the hollow without being recognised.

There are other characters who prowl through the countryside with slung rifles, jackets unbuttoned and caps askew. They have a look in their eyes which make them different from the rest. You know them immediately. They're the ones who carry on the war. They're indestructible. They drift around, game for anything. Danger attracts them, they love brushing with death. It's rare that such a man is caught. He's too quick, too skilful, too resolute. He masters the game and plays it for a long time. Then he breaks the rules once too often or he meets his match. There was a sergeant-major who had knocked out twenty-eight tanks in close combat; then he walked up to the commander of the twenty-ninth with only his pistol in his hand. He was a second too late. They fired at the same instant and both were killed.

Such men are often difficult to handle in back areas, but at the front, if rightly handled by the right officer, they can turn a company into a first-rate fighting unit because their bold resolution and aggressive spirit transfers itself to all the rest. Courage is infectious, just like cowardice.

In the evening there were long reports of enemy activity. They added up to a complete picture. The attack was expected. It began at 0030. The enemy opened up with everything he'd got, blinding the O.P.s, plastering the gun positions, concentrating his bombardment on our bridgehead at R. Almost at once the land-lines went dead; the report of the attack came over the wireless. Reception was poor. We put up a barrage blindly, going by the sound of battle which was thickening-up round R.

At dawn we stood outside and watched the dark smoke of the shell-bursts at the edge of the wood creeping towards our firing position. On the gun-sites one man was wounded. About a hundred and twenty Medium shells fell round the O.P. We put the weight of the whole barrage at about eight hundred to a thousand rounds, but actually there are said to have been nearly two thousand, half of them on R. Our own losses were small, and later on the O.P. reported that the assault on R. had been broken up by the fire of our battery.

The supply echelon arrived at 0400. At 1400 we entrained in the wind and rain. The approach to the railhead was by a corduroy road and there was a makeshift loading-ramp. The unwieldy Russian wagons were much damaged. The locomotive was a monster. The rain was slapping into the clay puddles and the wind howling in the telegraph wires. The gun crews were up to their arms and chests in mud. But without haste and without delay vehicle after vehicle rolled up the ramp; guns and limbers, signals wagons, office carts, forge, field kitchens and all the soft transport.

I can still remember how we shook our heads when we got the first local wagon, back in Kulm. It was a kind of rack-wagon such as peasants use for carting hay. We painted it grey to make it look a bit more military, but we were always ashamed of it and it had to travel right at the end of the column—the gypsy cart.

And today? Today all the movable possessions of an immense army are packed almost exclusively on these carts. The high box-carts which were once French ration wagons have been left behind long ago. The carts we possess have become even smaller; they're shabby, miserable little traps. But they go through any old mud, and if they bog down to the axles a pair of horses can get them out easily. With a hearty "All together now!" the gunners can lift a loaded trap and put it in its right place.

Next up the ramp went the horses, ten to a truck. Everything went smoothly, the battery is an old team. We were rolling westward. . . .

In R. we saw trains loaded with new guns and agricultural machinery, weapons of war and of peace. After all the destruction, one sensed the hand of order. Even the smallest station had something of a garden, with grass and trees and paths, and even where half the house had been blown away, the infantry had laid out little front-gardens of their own.

We were travelling down a corridor within range of enemy batteries. Once we saw two dark mushrooms two hundred yards from the track, but we could hardly hear the explosions because of the noise of the train. About day-break we heard the roar of diving aircraft, but the raid was on someone else.

Some time later Sergeant-Major Weise boarded the train. Meeting Sergeant Konrad, he asked him: "Has anything been happening?"—"Not a thing," answered Konrad, "—except last night we stopped another attack, a thousand rounds Medium. That's about all." Half an hour later the Sergeant-Major happened to be at Divisional Tactical Headquarters and heard the following: "Fantastic story! The Russians broke through with tanks and motorised infantry. Two thousand rounds fired in our sector. But 11 and 12 Batteries put up a good show." That's how a thing grows in geometrical progression according to the mileage from the front line.

We travelled to the end of the corridor, to the nail of the finger, so to speak, towards which another finger is reaching in an effort to close the circle. There's a gap of about eighty kilometres between them. But the enemy can't make much use of it, the country is against him. It's bare and monotonous. As far as one can see there's nothing but grassland with stunted trees and mixed woods. The miserable little villages on the hills look even sadder in the rain, as black as the marshland on which they are built. Even on the hills one's spade strikes water immediately in the moist, black marsh soil. The vehicles sink deep into the bog and we have to put four horses to each cart. They say the Russians have to carry their ammunition over thirty kilometres. We at least have the railway line as a backbone.

A strange war is being fought there with strong-points and armed convoys, small surprise attacks and no proper front line, air drops and ground strafing by aircraft. Altogether it's rather lame, with neither side putting on a show. It seems that the Russians can't, and we don't want to. A wagtail is nesting in a gun cradle of the heavy battery which we're relieving.

At two o'clock I went back with the empty train to Smolensk and Minsk on a duty journey. I found myself a place in the straw, which smelled of horses. From Vyasma I travelled in a German corridor coach. I reached Smolensk after twenty-four hours. At nine o'clock I found Henning. It wasn't easy. First I went through the back yard of a workshop; then through a garden. At the bottom I saw someone standing and shielding his eyes with his hand. It was a great meeting.

On July the 11th at eleven o'clock I started for Minsk. I reached the airfield in a Mercedes film-car. I couldn't get an aircraft but a field-car gave me a lift. Later I changed to a lorry and towards six in the evening I fetched up at an OT[1]-camp between Orsha and Borissov. A clean room, a well with clear, ice-cold water, and twenty minutes later I was just in time for a stage-show by a Russian company which called itself "Dosvidania" ("Good-bye").

The end of our first year. It hardly affects us. We mention it casually, half smiling. No cause for rejoicing, no cause for sadness. A day like any other. It's not worth talking about.

[1] Todt Organisation.

We are part of this war. It's a natural phenomenon. It was born and grew up, and when it wears out it will die. At first it was we who carried it along; now it's the war which carries us. We gave it a start, but in the end it has entered into us and made us its creatures. It has burnt out many things that were in us, and it will go on taking them away from us until we are reborn by it. It's wrong to fight against it; you mustn't look back, it only makes you sad and sick at heart. The only thing is to yield your soul to its power and make your peace with it. It's still stronger. But it will pass, like the rain.

30th of June, 1942. For eight days I have been drifting through the country from the hopeless parts to the better ones, and from the better ones to those that are really good—as far as such places exist in time of war. There's hardly a vehicle by road or rail which I haven't used. At first it was as if life were at a standstill. The goods train crawled through the countryside, and afterwards the regular military train took seven hours to do sixty kilometres. The landscape outside was always the same. How tired I've become of these dirty roads. One can't bear to see it any more, the rain, the ankle-deep mud, the eternal sameness of the villages. One doesn't want even to know their names. And then these small, dreary towns, whose single cobbled road goes as far as the station and no further. Even if one wanted to do something about it, it would only make sense if there were peace.

It became better towards Smolensk. I spread some straw on the floor of an open goods wagon, the sun was shining and I slept comfortably under my groundsheet. That was the evening I found Henning. I had looked at the wonderful ikons in the cathedral on my last visit. Otherwise there wasn't much to see in the ruined town, which once had one of the biggest universities as well as thirty-four grammar schools and technical colleges. In the cathedral they are now holding services again after an interruption of five years.

Apart from that, how should I describe Smolensk? Some

scenes stay in your mind when you look at them closely: emigrants, refugees, women and adolescents with bundles on their backs. There were hundreds of them in a ragged column, with a loud-speaker which would suddenly break into solemn, deafening music above their heads. Here there was a face with well-cut features, there some fine, clean-shaven heads above snow-white *rubashkas* with narrow belts and dark riding breeches. Sometimes there was a beautiful girl going on her way, quietly dressed, not looking left or right. Such sights are exceptions, but they make you think. When I was driving out to the airfield, we met a column of prisoners, apathetic, with the dull look of the defeated in their eyes. On the other side of the road women were standing and crying. It's not often that one sees tears: generally it's not part of the Russian character. Henning told me a story to illustrate it.

They had a woman to do the cleaning, and her brother helped her. The brother stole and was found out. After a summary trial he was shot. They didn't tell the woman, but she knew it. When someone happened to ask her about Vassil, she said: "Vassil potsh" (Vassil head off). She found it quite natural and shrugged her shoulders. Later, when she was told: "You be careful, nix potsh," she said quietly: "Nitchevo—voina" (it's war, so many die).

I strolled through the streets, looking at the girls, at the life in the squares and the many churches. Sometimes I sat on a bench in the park where children were playing. Once I took a droshky to see more of the city. There was something unreal in being a guest, a stranger in an already strange town. There was a mess where the Russian waiter said in German: "Beer, sir?" every time he put down another glass of vodka. Then there was a chapel over an archway with a black madonna. On high feast-days she's dressed up in stiff, glittering gold, surrounded by candles, to greet the bustling crowds below.

After a wearying journey I reached Minsk in an ammunition train at half-past two in the morning. At half-past three I climbed over a fence and found my old comrade Julius of the butcher company. For breakfast he slapped half a pound of butter, three quarters of a pound of black pudding and seven eggs into the frying-pan—I could hardly manage it.

In the afternoon I went on to Borissov, where ten hours' sleep helped me to recover from the fatigue of the journey and a cold in the head. I quartered myself in a small clean house, where I had stopped once before. It was during the advance. I had halted to wash off the road, and I liked it very much. At first the family was not too happy about my second visit. But after a while a shy smile appeared and we gained confidence in each other, the quiet shy woman, the wrinkled old *babushka*, and little Panyeka, who's fourteen years old. It's easy enough, if one treads carefully, showing a little friendliness to people and trying to put the war out of the way. I couldn't understand an officer who said to me a few days ago: "We can't afford to worry about the civilians' feelings, we have to get on with the war." As if the one excluded the other.

In the soldiers' hostel in S. I waited for the mail courier from Berlin. Outside there was a cloud-burst. It was a relief after the closeness of the last days. The night before had been so hot that I sweated from every pore. A land of extremes. Nothing happens in moderation. Heat and cold, dust and mud. Everything vehement and elemental. Why should one expect its people to be different?

Some Russian auxiliary police were sitting at my table, young Ukrainians and Galicians. Some of them were still wearing their brown tunics with hammer-and-sickle brass buttons, others had German uniforms without badges, and Russian belts—it was a crazy mixture. But they are good fellows, bold and reckless and good haters. Just what we need.

There was a lot of building going on in the town. The Bolsheviks had burnt down all the houses; only the skeletons were standing. Some was bomb damage, but elsewhere it was incendiarism. Now the buildings were being put in order again.

Roofs, floors, walls, staircases, windows, doors, balconies—everything being made like new. The base workshops and supply companies must have good billets for the winter.

12th of July, 1942. Back with the old mob. How glad I was to see the little valley again with the river and the good old dugouts in the hillside. "So you've arrived," said the Battery Commander. "We wondered if something had happened to you." And I felt like the prodigal son. Perhaps it's difficult to understand, but already the last bit of the journey felt like coming home. There was the big mine crater, the burnt-out wagons, the shell-holes right and left of the railway, the wrecked aircraft, the last loading-ramp and finally the entraining-officer's shack. It was all so familiar, as familiar as the voice of the front at night, as the light from the dugouts shining at the end of the road. Now I'm at peace again.

I had heard reports that something was happening on our sector, that we had had to shorten the line and divide the pocket, and it had worried me. But it's all right, nothing has altered, the movement was on our left. The only change is that Budde has been wounded, made up to sergeant, decorated with the Iron Cross (First Class), and packed off home.

The boys crowded into my dugout. A pale evening sky was shining through the muslin curtains of the window and I was reading. I got a letter from Jo, who's in the South, and another from Martin in the North; I was deeply moved. How scattered my friends are—in every theatre of the war: in Norway, in front of Leningrad, in Army Group Centre, in the Donetz basin, in Southern France, in Greece and Africa, on the coasts, on occupied islands, in the desert, on steppes and in forests, amid white mountains and within the walls of foreign cities—and yet they speak with the same voice; their hearts beat with the same rhythm.

There's Martin writing . . . I can see him drinking and thumping his fist on the table: "If only one could live again, and get on with one's work. I won't give up my dreams yet, we'll make it in the end. . . . I've found some beautiful ikons. . . . Here's to the future! . . . Now I'm rather drunk. . . ."

And there's Jo, sitting outside his house and writing about these odd times: "On a spider's thread hanging from the eaves, a straw is turning in the wind. The cat, Pyotr Junior, is sitting on the edge of a chair in the sunshine. It's late on Sunday morning (above seven a.m.). The gentle blue smoke of the kitchen range is drifting through the trees, and the clouds cast great shadows over the landscape. It's wonderful. Pale blue shot with yellow-white and pink; that's the colour scale in which I live at the moment. Perhaps it's a reward for the terrible first half of May, when the tanks broke through here. We twice re-took the power-station, and the valley was so black with smoke that one couldn't see the sky. Our garden of crosses got bigger and bigger, and when all the noise and confusion was over, I again had the sad task of lettering the white wooden boards. Now they're already growing grey beneath the hanging irises."—So writes Jo.

Here at the battery a fine rain is glittering in the evening sun, the air is very clear and a gentle light lies over the grass. I have just taken a deep breath. There are flowers on the slope by our dugout and on the table inside. It's light and friendly inside like a parlour.

Three hundred and fifty Russians have broken through and are moving about somewhere in the countryside. Towards evening there were sounds of shooting in the rear. The guards are being doubled. But it can't disturb God's peace.

Since yesterday I have been in the O.P. I went up to the old look-out to see how the country had changed. I walked through a meadow white with yarrow and marguerites and found a sunny slope with wild strawberries. I stayed so long there that they got worried. I couldn't tear myself away. My greed for those strawberries was enormous. There they were, red and ripe and heavy; you had only to stretch out your hand and stuff your mouth full. I threw off my cap and belt, and knelt down to pick them. Soon my hands were red. Then I went up to L. There were a lot of new shell craters, and a dugout had had a direct hit.

As I got nearer, there was the sound of a terrific battle. Next moment I saw a crowd of our boys doing a frenzied dance in their steel helmets, chucking hand-grenades and making a fantastic scene generally. They seemed to be using every possible means to agitate the Russians.

It turned out that the Divisional Commander had come up to L., that's to say, he was sitting at company headquarters wondering whether to venture any further forward. The boys had set up a Russian machine-gun and were firing at their own platoon headquarters. They were sad when he didn't come in the end. With great care they had also laid a trip-wire to a mine, hoping he'd blow it up. Now they blew it up themselves, setting fire to a barn in the process.

When the Great Man had gone, it immediately became quiet. Great guns, how we laughed.

Now it's midnight and I'm sitting and writing by candle-light. Outside the machine-guns are rattling, and behind me someone has just cried out in his sleep: "Ten rounds repeat! What was the elevation, sir?—7100. . . ." Then he turned over with a sigh. Not far away, if you go outside, you can see the flares above the new line which has closed the great pocket.

Chapter VIII

"HERE WE ARE, COMRADES"

In August 1942 the Russians launched a heavy attack on the Central Sector, particularly against Rzhev. It came at an awkward moment, for several of the armoured divisions of Army Group South, having reached Maikop and the outskirts of the Caucasus, were ironically halted for want of fuel. At the same time, there was a nervous move to reinforce the Atlantic Coast defences after the Canadian landing at Dieppe. In the desperate fighting which follows, Pabst's division was called to the relief of another German formation overrun by the Russians.

RAIN. It's been falling all night and all day. The duck-boards outside our house flap into the puddles under our feet. But there's one advantage: we don't get called on for patrols. Also the flies are peaceful—the flies which leave their filth on everything and everybody, and rise up in thick clouds whenever you take a garment from the wall by the stove.

The evening is very quiet. There's a mist over the low-lying land, and the roofs of houses seem to be floating in the pale light. Somewhere a cart is creaking, the horses stamp in the stables, there's a clink of chains. The country is wide and calm, as if the front were holding its breath for a while.

You're remote from all worries sitting here in a blockhouse in the middle of a swampy wood, surrounded by the machine-gun emplacements each of which is connected with the next by narrow duck-boards. The sentries are silent; they don't take risks—there's too much rabble drifting about in the wood. We had to shoot a fire lane through the wood to create the necessary space between the enemy and ourselves. All this is a different world. I'm grateful for it.

In times like these the front is the best place to be. Not that there is always a great deal of work here. Sometimes there's very little, and a man has to learn how to be alone with himself. I like it. At the front you are utterly free: free from petty cares and moods, from hopelessly resisting things which cannot be altered. Just as a military order is short and precise, so there are no doubts about our task, no problems beyond day-to-day affairs. Apart from a few things we all have in common, such as the wish to go home again one day and the thought of those whom we love, we have left everything behind us. We have no time to think about other matters or to get involved.

Here I can walk through the wood feeling only the bliss of the green half-light after the blinding sun in the clearing. I can sit at the massive entrance of my blockhouse, enjoying the smell of resin and the warmth of the summer day, which floods the wood with great waves of scent of the meadows.

The sickness of our time can be put into a few formulas. It strikes me that one can think about it much better out here, where it's not obscured by the noise of every-day life, and one's not cut off from calm reflection by wishful thinking. For here we are free even of wishes. They have become too pointless before the un-certain morrow. Nothing stands between us and the great march of events.

Towards 2 a.m. somebody came in shouting "Get up!" By three o'clock the advance party was already moving off on the black, boggy roads, through the steaming swamp, and the country of flat hills and dark villages. I am always affected by this land-scape with its vastness and the enormous sweep of its economical lines. This morning there was nothing but the dark ribbon of the road, the green of the grassland almost equally dark in the cool light, the shallow drifts of mist among the hills, and the villages floating on the crests. There was no variety, no charm. A single, severe tone dominated everything, so that a solitary horseman might be swallowed up and at the same time remain visible from afar like a thing apart. A gun-carriage got bogged and for a while there was nothing amid the hills but a bunch of gunners, horse-teams, tow ropes and hoisting gear round the ungainly vehicle and a loud, imperative "All together, heave!"

The battery stretched out along the road. From the hills you could see the vehicles wending their way forward up gradients and round bends. Then came the usual entraining drill. Shoulder to shoulder, beautifully co-ordinated. Then we rolled eastward and during the many halts we would talk or swear good-naturedly, the laughter rippling from wagon to wagon.

I slept a little on a pile of hay beneath our cart.

We are glad of the sun, of this interlude when one's will may go to sleep, when everything is arranged for us and we are merely shifted to where we are needed. We cursed the work, the up-heaval, the new moving about, because it's man's nature to be stationary and lazy. But we have already accepted and forgotten it. Soon we shall be building new emplacements, not for the first time and not for the last; we'll do what's needed and we'll soon feel at home. It won't require much since we're really nomads. Then we'll live in the present again and all this will be just an-other past episode.

We rode into the uncertain night, which was filled with the roar of engines. Parachute flares were dropping from the clouds. The earth shook with heavy explosions. There was the sparkle of incendiary bombs. Flak, a rocket-launcher flashing in the darkness, artillery duels. The whole arena was framed by a semi-circle of shivering signal lights, which was constantly being renewed with its silent message: "Here we are, comrades, here we are!"—the cry of the far-flung firing line. We continued our ride towards it. Mud shone dully like lead in the light of the flares, hard roads echoed to the clatter of hooves, there were the ruins of a dead town where the only living things were the sweetish-smelling fires and ourselves—the masters of this land, so far from the other one where women and children live.

We rode on into the morning. I did the same journey three times; there was nothing but the creaking of saddles and the clink of stirrups. There came the hour of complete indifference when one was blind and deaf, unable to think of anything but sleep. Then came the other hour—the moment when one could go down to a stream and revive oneself, when one felt a little better except that one's eyes were still half closed and sensitive to the light, and one's throat was parched with an unassuageable dryness.

My pony whinnied towards the morning. He is always whinnying. You can tell him far away. He's small and sturdy. His voice is hoarse and rough, and when he uses it his ugly mug reminds me of those studies by Leonardo da Vinci, which are so repulsive and yet so powerful.

There isn't an hour of the day which isn't filled with the roar of fighters and Stukas. A Ju 87 came flying back low overhead. Full of high spirits, it switched on its diving-siren. Our horses went wild, but all the same we appreciated the comradely greeting. There is always a strong, instinctive joy when two different arms meet in a combined operation. The pilots wave from above and we look up and wave back.

We rode into the new area, splashed with mud and water up to our ears. Mosquitoes hung on the horses' necks like round, red rubies. When we came back from the new O.P., the gun echelon was just bringing up the last piece. The cries of the drivers echoed through the hollow between two villages. In the background the conflagration went on. Enormous columns of smoke were rising into the sky, dark, white and violet, constantly fed by the merciless shelling which shook the earth and rattled the windows. Squadrons of our own planes and the enemy's were cutting across each other in the air. Ours were more numerous. A Russian bomber disintegrated in a sharp explosion, and burning wreckage rained down from the smoke-cloud.

22nd of August, 1942. 0700. For an hour and a half now we've been under drum-fire: rocket salvoes, heavy mortars, tanks. Five

93

fighter-attacks. Tanks broke through on our left. Direct hit on the O.P. Telephone shot to pieces, otherwise no casualties. Fire control moved into our personnel dugout. Several tanks in front of our position, all burning. Have prepared concentrated charges; within reach are hand-grenades and the machine-pistol. The main attack is on the neighbouring sector, five hundred yards to the left.

0730. Fiendish barrage. Flat in a crater with mud all over my back. Mortars and Stalin organ.

0800. Infantry attacking at northern edge of wood. Barrage "Ludwig". Enemy battery changes position on slope to the south-west—B Red has no more ammunition. Fire with Rosenberger 3.

0820. Our own battery in action again: delayed-action fuses, all guns take on infantry at edge of wood!

0825. The Stukas at last. Out with the signal pistols: indicate target.

0830. Hooray, they're diving!

0835. Fighter-bombers join in: bombs and machine-guns. Visibility impaired by the explosions. Over in the Russian lines the first casualties are going back.

0900. Company advancing in south-west corner B.—Now there are two companies, horse artillery, motor transport. Fire order: Base-line direction 235 plus, elevation 7200. Three hits.

0930. Infantry attacking through barrage Ludwig with tank support.

1020. They almost had us. But for the past twenty minutes the wood before us has been under a rain of bombs. A heavy one dropped 200 yards from the main gun line. The earth heaved up. The wood is covered with enormous clouds from the explosion.

1025. Ratas attacking. Our fighters got four of them in three minutes.

1030. Tanks again. Anti-tank guns firing like mad.

1035. Watch out, fighters! New attack. A message says: "Tank hit." Our small gun's third victim today.

1037. New target concentration at B. Fifteen horse-drawn wagons and a company. Fire order: Charge No. 6. Impact-fuses, all guns!

1045. On the left our Stukas. Ratas to our front. Behind us Tabrakova is burning furiously, black and red.

1100. Fourth tank hit by our 50-mm. anti-tank gun; the 76 got a couple more. All together thirteen on the battalion sector.

1200. The line to the firing position was in order for exactly five minutes today. Then it was shot to pieces again. Now it's melting in the fire in Tabrakova. We go on firing by wireless: "Hello, Red One! Pass your message."

1220. That's the fourteenth tank burning out; the fifth to our small anti-tank gun. The big gun suffered a direct hit and was overrun. Two tanks broke through but the eighty-eights got them in front of T. A deserter. The Russians only arrived yesterday from Moscow. They're calling up everybody between fourteen and fifty. A few days ago we caught one aged only thirteen.

1530. The battle is getting quieter. The Stukas are flying their sixth or seventh sortie. The tanks have retreated into the wood. Our shooting resulted in some wonderful tree bursts; they have a frightful fragmentation effect. There are supposed to be four hundred men in the wood to our front. Probably they have had enough for the moment.

1600. A rocket carpet—right on top of us. The dust and the stench. We made ourselves flatter still. Cries of "Pabst?"— "Meissner?"—"O.K. Go on firing." Our third round scored a beautiful direct hit on a gun position.

1645. Line-men came back with the news that our man of few words, General Rittau, had been killed.

In the evening, quiet. Traversing machine-gun fire. The Russians were towing their tanks away. Others we blew up. We stood together at company headquarters, talking about the

General. People used to curse him because he demanded so much. Now they say he was the Division itself. And it's a good Division. He was taciturn and had an iron calm. They say the food was bad at Division. Whenever he was served with a special dish, he would look at it silently for a while and then ask: "Is that what my infantry are having?"—That was our General.

24th of August, 1942. 0415. Third day of battle. It's just starting, on the ground and in the air simultaneously.

0445. For an hour and a half there's been fiendish drum-fire in the sector on the left. Yesterday morning at 0030 I came back to the firing position for two days' relief, but last night I had to go up again. Lieutenant D. had been killed. Spengler has been wounded. Direct hit on the look-out.

During the night we built a dugout.

I don't know what time it is; both my watches have succumbed to the effects of the battle. I only know that the shelling has been going on since 0445, and one wouldn't believe a few square yards of earth could withstand so much iron.

0700. A short breathing space. Not so much shelling. We have got two dugouts, one for the look-out, the other for our wireless operator, eighty yards to the rear. Between the two there have been some shells. They have wrecked our cable. 120 mm. One of them fell three yards from the wireless dugout and ripped the beam over Christiner's entrance to shreds. Lieutenant Mack and I look like niggers. We crawled through the cabbage plot to mend the cable. Telephone communication was impossible in all this noise. They made a mortar attack just as I had got halfway up. The rocket carpet came down as I was lying in the crater of the 120.

The new look-out was just finished by morning. It's a miserable burrow and rather damp. We have to crouch. Ten minutes at the telescope makes you stiff in the neck. But we're glad we've got so far. Tonight we'll make improvements.

"I'll be glad when evening comes," Christiner just said to me on the telephone. So will I. So far today our little anti-tank gun has bagged five tanks. Yesterday the regimental score was fifty-eight. One broke through today where Franz Wolf was sitting with his signallers in the sector on the left. Yesterday we shook hands in passing. At battalion headquarters they told me that two days before he had just had time to send a message: "Tanks!—F . . . ing off!" then he ran for it, headphones and everything hanging round him. He hadn't heard the tanks till they were ten yards away.

They've been attacking here now since the beginning of July. It's incredible. They must be having frightful losses. Every yard of ground is bitterly contested. Day after day we break up their assembly areas. They seldom manage to deploy their infantry even within reach of our machine-guns. We see the bomb craters, we see them drag in their wounded, their tanks get stopped, their aircraft crash. They run about frightened and helpless when we drop our heavy shells in front of their noses. But then they come on again in open order and move into the woods where they get plastered by our artillery and the Stukas. Of course we have losses too, but they can't be compared with the enemy's.

1800. I'm guessing the time from the sun. New attack. It's on the left again. The tanks are rolling in to the attack, and how! You can hear them quite distinctly; you can almost see them grind forward, and predict to the second when they'll reach our lines and start barking. But already our artillery is on the job. The wood is covered with fire-red shell-bursts and dark clouds of smoke. Machine-guns are rattling. The fragmentation effect must be frightful. Meanwhile far behind us the anti-tank guns opened up, but it only lasted between fifteen and thirty minutes. Then it got quiet. Now we can hear the noise of a new wave of tanks. Nothing happening so far. For seconds not a single shot. Hold your fire, let them come close! In the telescope a burning house—the smoke of shelling drifting away like mist. No visible movement on the enemy's side.

97

A little later, in the evening twilight, hell broke loose once more: mortars, tanks, machine-guns. But of all the attacking infantry only a couple of deserters reached our lines. Then it calmed down and we spent a second night building up our dugout. Now it has a good roof, a cushioning layer of bricks and an earth buffer against ricochets. We have also dug a crawling trench between the two dugouts.

24th of August, 1942. The day started early with fighter strafes. Otherwise it has belonged to the rocket-launchers, whose white firing cloud goes up every hour above the enemy's lines behind the wood. A few tanks and mortars have sent us a mixed morning mail-bag, but on the whole it's quiet and there's little movement on the enemy's part. We have even been outside a couple of times to sun ourselves at the back of the dugout: two spells of about five minutes.

It's a strange sight as you stand at the dugout entrance for a moment. The boys are dispersed in their holes, behind shattered garden fences, in haystacks, among the weeds of overgrown fields, in the ruins of burnt houses. Sometimes you catch sight of one as he doubles across the road, the momentary shine of a steel helmet. They're always at the ready, quick to dive for cover. You can hear the click of the machine-gun breeches, sometimes a short shout. Generally it's quiet in the pauses between the firing. But you can feel the tenseness.—Tonight I shall be relieved.

At dusk I was on my way back. The last squadrons rushed over the woods with howling sirens. The fires became more noticeable, the explosions more erratic. There was a wild sea of spraying tracer, the salvoes of the Stalin organ, and the red, green and white flares, rising majestically into the soft evening sky.

Later on we were inundated with canteen rations, so I was able to offer Franz Wolf a schnapps. Suddenly we were all together and it was good to see their honest old faces again. There's always something wonderful about finding one another alive. Meissner was there waiting to go up as a relief. Christiner said: "Haven't they got you yet, old man? No? Well, you're lucky."—"They've ripped a hole in my jacket," said Franz, "I've just had it patched up."—"So what, look at my pistol holster," said Meissner. We all agreed that one felt pretty naked lying up there. "But not when you're with the mob," said Christiner. "When you're with the mob you don't care what happens. And you wouldn't want to be with any other lot. When I came back from leave, I found the Eleventh, but when they told me the battery was on its way, everything was all right.—And with things as they are? Well, what the hell. Times may change."

Just at the moment the battery is doing a rapid shoot—the second this evening. The black smoke of the flash-reducing charge means that you only occasionally see a jet of flame. The breech-blocks slam dully, the cartridge cases tinkle out, then you hear the signallers again: "Hello, Red Two . . . nothing to report here." Clear and precise, yet almost sing-song. You sense how everything works together—the observers up ahead, the signallers, the guns.

Since yesterday I have been in the forward area again. No sleep last night. Enemy shelling one moment, our own artillery the next. We have strengthened our dugout still more. Today was quieter. Dust and smoke are still drifting in through the entrance, but unless a beam gets displaced or a great lump of earth falls into the dixie, we don't pay much attention.

It's getting towards evening. My steel helmet feels heavy and my tongue is numb from smoking so much. The sun slants into the dugout. How good a sip of wine is.

I held up the dusty bottle in the shimmering, sun-lit smoke and enjoyed the play of colours, green and red. Wasn't there a Spanish madonna with a cloak like that?

My companion by my side is flat out. In sleep his face is pale and pinched. I can see the stubble on his chin. We have a Russian cloak which we wrap round our legs and pull right over our ears whenever we can. Only one of us actually sleeps at a time, but on a cold night it's big enough for two.

A little later Lieutenant Mack and Class arrived, and Hans and I went back. We tightened the straps of our steel helmets and hurried. It's not a very cosy feeling waiting for the bullets as you walk on a moonlit night across a bare hill. We wanted to put it behind quickly, to be over the innumerable shell-holes, the flattened, burnt and churned-up cornfield in front of T., the cratered crossings, the roads with their yawning pits. A sentry by the anti-tank gun challenged us softly. Then there was the knocked-out tank and afterwards the dip where we always light a cigarette.

Once again I was looking at target-point 215. There were some flak positions on a road-crossing. A man appeared in the open, took off his coat, stood in his shirt-sleeves in the bright sunshine, then strolled casually to a water-hole to have a wash. "Reinhard," I said, "Reinhard, just look at that, isn't that some cheek?" We were squatting there with itching fingers. If only some vehicles were to come along! But the God of war was kind. Two vehicles actually appeared. They came trotting briskly over the hill by point 235 and made towards 315. What luck! Out went the fire order: "... report when ready for action ... Fire!" We waited— there it was ... rrrumph ... and then the mushroom! Our Ivan was scared out of his wits: a 150-mm. shell is no Easter egg. He grabbed his jacket and vanished into his hole, leaving a trail of dust. The drivers turned their horses and galloped away. We got them again at 325. One of the horses turned driverless in circles and we felt better.

It was fun, Father. It heartened us, and I thought of your stories of the Beresina. Didn't you do that sort of thing yourselves? You would lie in wait and laugh: "Watch them jump!" you'd say. Mother always got angry at that: "What a sickening lot you men are!" But I knew just how you felt.

In the morning I was lying in my burrow with a slight temperature. I was dreaming of a restful sleep protected by motherly hands; a sleep in which I could let go of all the things which make me so tense—like this constant being on call. A sleep from which I might wake up smiling, a sleep which wasn't one long, restless dream. As it is, ever since four o'clock the soil has been crumbling through the straw revetting of the dugout roof: sometimes it falls quite copiously, as if the rafters were shaking themselves. At times I wondered whether to turn round and lie with my head to the entrance, where there might be more room if it came to the worst. But dazed by the fever I felt too indifferent. I merely curled up more tightly. At eight o'clock there were ten hits round our little group of dugouts. The beams and groundsheet over my entrance are in shreds, the motor-cycle which was standing there is useless, and a fragment went through my ration box, covering the contents with sawdust.

During the afternoon both sides stepped up their air activity. From every direction the big kites sailed in towards the heart of the battle with fighters circling round them. For half an hour we watched attacks and pursuits going on at three different levels. A formation of Stukas dived down close by a Russian fighter squadron: they dropped from the sky undaunted, one plane after another. High overhead the anti-aircraft shells were searching after their prey, while down below fighters followed hard on the tail of fire-spitting bombers. It seems as if the efforts of whole armies and airfleets is slowly becoming concentrated on this dirty little piece of soil. It went on deep into the night. Northwards the cloud-banks were lit with the usual fires; ahead of us the battle-field was ringed by muzzle-flashes, and the earth groaned with the slam of explosions. Over it all hung a sky with cold, flickering stars. Sometimes you can't believe that life can survive in this zone. And yet it does, in thousands of human beings, feverish, watchful, determined to survive.

Yesterday the enemy began his drum-fire at four o'clock again.

But it wasn't long before our Stukas got on to him. We attacked with some local successes against tenacious resistance. The battery was in action all through the night. This morning the Nebelwerfers joined in. Hosemann was on his way with the dixie to fetch coffee when it started. He stood rooted to the ground. "Jesus," he said, "the lions' cage is open!" It really is a hellish, hideous roaring when the rockets go off.

Flanders came back from leave yesterday. He said (and he spoke for everyone who goes on leave): "Nineteen months is a long time, though I know that some people have had to wait even longer. I felt quite shy when I walked through the town, no exaggeration. You're no longer used to it. There are big stone buildings, and broad streets, and gardens and parks. It's all so unreal, as if you don't belong there any more. Then you reach your home . . . to think that it still exists! The sofa, where you can stretch out with a book, the reading-lamp, the radio . . . and there's no shooting, none at all. . . ."

It's night-time. I'm lying in my hole with a temperature and writing between spasms of coughing. There's a movement outside—footsteps—a call: "Hello, still up?" Edu appears. He comes back from the forward area, caked with dirt and sprouting a stubbly beard. He stretches out across my legs and says: "Boy, what a time we had! Dugout collapsed. A one-seventy. We were half buried, but everyone's all right. Five times Ivan meant to attack, five times there was an artillery preparation, and five times his infantry didn't budge. The place is practically flat. Had to dig out the machine-guns. Do you happen to have a drink?"

CHAPTER IX

IN THE OLD FIRING POSITION

In the autumn of 1942 the pattern of disaster was already being set in the South. Kleist's armour made a new and unsuccessful attempt to push into the Caucasus from Mozdok, leaving the Army Group with an exposed flank of a thousand miles. Meanwhile the battle for Stalingrad —originally an easy objective, had it been attacked with address— continued to draw off the German reserves. On the Central Sector, however, the Russian summer offensive had been held, and in September Pabst's unit found itself back in its old position.

WE were talking about whether it was good to have something to hold on to during the drum-fire. One thing we found was that the atheists have a more difficult time of it, because there are moments when the personal power of resistance dies in you. At times like that it's good if a man has some other power to give him strength. That's why one shouldn't destroy the faith of a believer. For the same reason it's not always the young men who are the most reliable, though you can never tell in advance. It's always been proved that you can't judge a man properly until you've seen him under fire. There are some who become almost debonair, they develop a sense of humour in the most impossible situations. These are the salt of the earth.

Despite your self-control, I can read your secret anxiety in all your letters. What actually is my attitude to death? One tries to avoid discussing these questions. Death is always present here, so much present that we can't overlook it. For that reason we have long ago defined our attitude towards it. Some people fear death greatly. They cling to the hope that it will pass them by in the crowd. Thus they are torn between hope and fear. They pale in the face of danger.

Most people simply don't think about it. They exclude it from their consciousness. It'll be all right, they think; and they try to take their chance without avoiding danger more than their duties permit.

Death in battle is not a natural death. It's true that the opposite theory is the cornerstone of Quinton's teaching. Quinton was not right about this. To give one's life for the sake of one's country, to die so that manhood may live on in the consciousness of the race—that's not our only vocation. What matters is that the willingness to die is not extinguished, because a people whose men have forgotten how to die is doomed to decline.

But it is also true that each of us has still much to hope for, to strive for and desire; much that goes beyond a sudden death. We carry unborn works within us which want to be created. It's just in these years, when all our abilities except the military ones lie fallow, that we want to do so many things still. To fulfil his life's work is another of the tasks, and not the smallest one, which a man owes to his country.

So it seems to me that we're not meant to accept death as something natural, a mere matter of course. That would mean we should be extinguished in advance, that no other thought would guide us, that without this last fulfilment our lives would be futile.

Death on the battlefield is a noble fulfilment of a man's life, but it's not the only one. The loss to his race and country can be repaired. We are all expendable, even the best of us. New generations will be born, and in them all our strength and abilities will be reincarnate so long as men know how to die. The sources of a nation are inexhaustible. The individual must fight on in the knowledge that his own fulfilment may be possible.

If you risk your life, to regain it daily with heightened value, if you rub shoulders with death, because it's exciting to gamble with the last stake, you allow for death as a natural part of your life, and even in death you will find the satisfaction of having got the better of it for so long. If the dangerous life is only a phase —and a trace of its glamour sticks to every man—then death in battle is but one of many possibilities. It's a premature end; you will not accept it with indifference, but you can accept it with equanimity. You can face it with calm and composure, with the dignity which goes with a conscious attitude to life, and with the will to do your worst against the foe, to sell your life dearly, to do your duty grimly to the last.

But it's not so much the thought of our own death which moves us, but fear of the death of those whom we love. We feel sure of our own strength, and boast of having escaped death. You feel equal to the danger which you can look in the eye; even if it proves too powerful to withstand, the wave of darkness which floods over our consciousness is brief. And once danger is past, we give ourselves over to living again.

On these moonlit nights a transparent mist hangs among the fir trees and the silver grass crackles under one's feet. Our second winter is approaching. I'm sure that the lessons of the first will help us. But we shall need courage and tenacity more than ever, as well as the strength to live without illusions. Because it's a thankless job we're doing. Here we must stand or fall. It's a war without mercy.

25th of September, 1942. It's just as it was last year when we were in front of Byely, when we made our first hole in a wall and built a chimney with sods of turf. Since then we have made some progress: we ram a number of tins into one another or dismantle an exhaust-pipe from a shot-down Russian bomber. But the measurements of the fire-place have remained the same: one spade wide, one high, and two spades deep. The chimney always smokes at first. Then the earth dries out, the logs begin to crackle and we gaze into the fire reminiscing: "Way back . . . yes . . . do you remember? . . ."

105

Today I returned to the battery. At the entrance of the dugout, Schmuck was sitting with a pail of steaming potatoes. I took a couple and peeled off the thin skin. They were wonderful and hot, but it was only after I had strolled on that I realised how much I had enjoyed eating them. I was perfectly contented, and it occurred to me once again how grateful we have become for small things.

I'm doing forward observation duty again. I was to have relieved somebody further to the right, and the change of orders reached me when I was already on my way. We walked quite a bit that night with our kit and equipment, and walking's not so easy with a bundle on your back and another on your chest, with gumboots like frogmen's flippers, through mud and puddles and this wretched scrub where all the time you have to watch out that you don't lose direction. But every road ends somewhere. The position is being held by a Bavarian unit. The firing trench stretches across bare country. It's narrow and fairly dry on the hills, but in the hollows it's flooded and you have to splash through the muddy water. The machine-gun posts jut forward like small bastions. They command the ground in front, which is laced with hollows and strips of scrub. Everywhere there are knocked-out tanks. It's as if our position had acted as a breakwater to a wave, bringing it to a standstill like an enormous, stranded Armada. Here on the hill the position is well constructed. There are drains for water; the dirt gets caught and the water is clear enough to wash in and rinse out the mess tins. Short trenches lead to the latrines and refuse pits. A supply trench connects us with the rear. The only trouble is that because of the high water-level the dugouts are low. You have to crouch behind the parapet of the trench if you want to avoid attracting a bullet. There are two of us in one hole, and one can just crawl over the other. Sitting upright is impossible. Neither above or below, nor even sideways, is there a foot of room to spare. Every movement becomes a major operation. The floor is covered with straw. That's all we have, apart from the narrow shelf where we put our rations, and a recess for the

telephone. I have squeezed in the map-board and binoculars behind my head; everything else is outside. It's cold. We have put a
light between two herring-tins to warm some tea in a mug. When
we sleep, we pull the blanket over our heads and warm each other.

I walked round the position. The sun was shining. In a sheltered
corner the crew of the first machine-gun were catching lice
and scraping the mud off their coats with a knife. There was
occasional mortaring. One of them caught a packet. Blood began
to form a dark pool and he lay there groaning. His comrades were
holding up his head, carefully putting a mug to his lips. One
man talked to him as if he were talking to a child: "That's the stuff
—that'll do you good—be quiet now—sure—they'll come for you
in a moment—in a moment, Alfred, in a moment." At dusk I was
standing in the trench, testing the wireless. Something was
wrong. I twiddled a bit and suddenly I got the German shortwave
station. The Platoon Commander passed by and we shared the
earphones. Light opera. How strange it sounded. . . .

As soon as it got dark we started to build a new dugout. Slowly
the moon was rising. The brittle grass crackled underfoot.
The weapons were iced up. During a pause I walked over to
Sergeant-Major Rath, who was acting as the forward look-out to
my right. He had just come back from leave and I wanted to hear
if Frankfurt was still standing. Also I wanted to hear the story of
how he nearly landed in the opposite camp a few days ago.

"It was quite simple," he told me. "There I was, coming up
along the line of scrub. But I got on to the wrong line, the one
which goes through the boggy hollow and ends in the fighting
area. There was no trench, and I didn't see any bog; but I did see
some dugouts. I was just going towards my own, when somebody
called me. I couldn't understand him very well, his voice sounded
funny. I said: 'What's the matter?' And he said: 'Bradi, bradi.'
Damn, I thought, 'Brother, brother'? That can't be right. I
turned round smartly. Ten yards away, one of the ration carriers
asked me: 'Do you want us to come on, sir?' I ask you. . . .

When we were fifty yards away I said to the men: 'You silly ——s, couldn't you see they were Russians?' Ivan didn't fire a shot; it was incredible. But then they woke up in our own trench, and a pair of machine-guns started. I threw myself flat and kept calling out till someone shouted 'Here!' At last we got into the trench, but for a time they wouldn't believe we were Germans, the beggars."

I was standing by the first machine-gun, waiting for the artillery preparation which was to precede our attack. The programme started dead on time. Shortly afterwards the first squadron of Stukas appeared. The ground was covered with bursting shells of every calibre; the dark, grey-white smoke drifted up into a violet cloud moving slowly westward.

Sharp against the sunlight were the mushrooms of further hits. One after another they rose in strange shapes, sometimes like a cabbage stalk, sometimes with spurting spearheads, sometimes like a clenched fist. All the time the dive-bombers were plunging down into the smoke, and through the glasses you could see enormous lumps of earth being flung into the air. The barrage jumped forward towards the enemy's rear areas. First you could see individual men and then whole groups dashing backwards. But there were still the yellow muzzle flashes of the tanks, and again and again the cloud in the east which showed that a rocket carpet had been fired. Our batteries replied with a heavy barrage. By evening we had achieved our objective and the enemy had become visibly downcast.

My relief came up with a couple of vehicles carrying timber. It was so quiet that we could drive right up to the dugout. Everybody gave a hand. Posts and planking were piled up quickly and quietly, and soon the vehicles had vanished again like ghosts in the moonlight. At four we hung a groundsheet over the entrance and lit the first fire in the stove. At four-thirty we staggered back with heavy feet, terribly tired.

2nd of October, 1942. The advanced observer has reported two heavy mortar hits. The dugout is so badly damaged that it's no longer usable. No casualties. All our work gone to the devil. All right, we'll build a new one.

Evening. For the next month I'm to live in this dugout by myself. When I'm back with the battery, that is. I'm glad. I'm so happy being alone. This morning Edu woke me up, just because he wanted to chat, and I was still so tired. In the evening the lads creep in to tell me their troubles. Sometimes I have tactfully to get rid of them. I have so much to do, and when there's no more work, I would like to read a book sometimes. One can't always be giving. I want to toast my bread by myself and let my thoughts wander. Most people don't seem to share this need to be alone, but solitude never bored me.

In any case, I'm not really alone. There's the stove who sings his stories. And there's the mouse above me in the timber. They're my friends, with whom I talk.

Today the new dugout of the forward O.P. has been made ready for habitation, which probably accounts for the fact that with the final load of timber for a second roof, the relief brought news of an impending move.

We've been able to build in peace during these last three days. Nothing much happened. In fact, we scarcely ever smelled gunpowder. Anyway, our trench is deep. As for the characters who creep up at night with machine-pistols, and the traversing fire of the machine-guns, they're just pin-pricks. We're used to them and hardly even listen. A little Russian anti-tank gun blew one of our machine-gun posts to bits and shoved the earth from the parapet into the trench. But since the machine-gun is only there at night, we laughed. A pity I was in the neighbouring sector doing some ranging, or I'd have got him, the dirty little squirt. However, the next day I plastered him and he piped down. It was no great masterpiece of gunnery; we were only four hundred yards away from each other. But it was a lively moment, because the Russians had seen me and they got very busy. Luckily my fire order was already on its way and for the rest of the day we didn't see another sign of them.

These anti-tank guns are hard to catch. They change position all the time. They get pushed forward, fire a few rounds, and disappear before you know where you are. If you're not on the spot with a fire order ready you can't catch them.

I have been strolling along the line, enjoying the company of our bearded warriors. Some of them actually have beards, long beards which would do credit to a U-boat mate. They're irrepressible. "Well, look who's here, our artillery observer. Come here, my boy, I want to show you something. That's where you ought to put down some fire, just over there. And next time, boy, if you're not right there to give me twenty rounds, I'll come and warm up your dugout for you."—"Come on, let's tickle old Ivan's tail a bit; I've got the sniper's rifle. . . ." We lay down side by side, the one with binoculars, the other with the telescopic sight. . . .

Early one morning I walked through the trench and found a sentry—a little man with a round face beneath his steel helmet. He was standing there alone, hunched up with the cold, shifting from one leg to the other. Then another man slipped out of the dugout, a tall, lean fellow with a red beard. They greeted each other affectionately.

"Happen to have a cigarette left, old cock?" the little man asked. "Sure," said the tall one, beaming. "Wait a sec, I'll get it."

"You know," said the sentry, when the other had gone (and one felt he had to say it just once), "we're great pals, the two of us." His round face was radiant and he was happy I was there to see this great and wonderful thing. The tall one came back, and they leant together against the wall of the trench, sharing their cigarette between them. Look, I thought, there's no longer anything extraordinary in this idea that one man should go through fire for the other; it's quite simple and matter-of-course.

I drove back through pitch darkness. Rain sprayed into our faces. When we weren't sure of the way, the horses found it. I discovered my lonely dugout, together with my mail and a stack of wood left for me by a comrade.

It's our last evening in the dugout at the old gun position. My companion reads and I write. The stove is red hot. There has been an issue of schnapps; in the dixie is some water from the nearest puddle and we're going to make grog. I have only to reach between my knees to pick up fresh firewood. Everything's to hand, no need to budge. The mice in the boards are rattling and nibbling and throwing down dirt. Sometimes I pick up a piece of wood and put it through the holes, then it's quiet for a while. That's about the only thing which disturbs our peace.

Nothing can shake us any more. I don't say that in bravado but quietly and soberly, with a kind of indifference.

Come what may—it can hardly surpass what we have behind us. When I think about it, I would almost go so far as to say that the enemy is no longer capable of mounting such assaults. What worried us last winter was not so much the Russian infantry, but the special Siberian troops. Now we know from our experience here that he no longer has such troops. He has to make every assault with intense artillery preparation and massive use of armour if he hopes for any chance of success. Even then his infantry often fail to move. And what he hasn't achieved so far, he won't achieve in the coming winter. Perhaps he may break through here and there, but he won't have a lasting success. For us it remains a question of patience, perseverence and tenacity—none of them spectacular qualities, not the kind that you can make much noise about, but qualities which demand more in the end than does any attack.

Attack inspires, it produces the reckless fighter. Defence isn't glorious, but it makes you hard. It's harder to lie under fire waiting for an attack to come in than to storm through a curtain of fire and throw the enemy out. The attacker is drunk with excitement, he doesn't feel the danger. It is he who determines the course of action. The defender has to wait, he doesn't know what's coming. His resistance may be bitter but it's without enthusiasm.

It has been raining all day. It was raining when we were whistled out of bed at 4 a.m., it was raining when the guns left the limber positions, and when we followed with the battery detail and signal section. We overtook the guns and went ahead to take over the new position. Now it's 2000 hours. The guns haven't arrived, but the rain continues.

I was standing on the back seat of the wireless cart, holding a bad foot in the air and looking at my comrades with their clothes clinging tightly to their bodies. The rain and snow were drifting into their faces and an icy wind flapped through their wet ground-sheets. The drivers sat on the high seats of the wagons with frozen hands and unhappy faces; their heads hung to one side. Thus they drove through the dreary mud, furrowing their vehicles through water and swamp like clumsy, painfully loaded ships, stamping and swaying in the potholes and ruts of the *Roll-bahn*. The surface of logs was sometimes visible deep down in the mud and the drainage ditches were brimming over.

In the worst of the low-lying swamp a second layer of fascines had been laid on top like a plaster. Despite the binding, it was still so springy and full of bumps that one's soul was shaken out of one's body and it was a full-time job not to fall overboard. That's the *Rollbahn*, a straight, properly-edged track, the fruit of much hard work in contrast to the other roads, which are like rushing streams. But sometimes even the *Rollbahn* spills over its edges. It happens on the slopes, where the carts slew sideways and the drivers have to feel their way by probing if they are to gain safe ground without damage.

On such a slope a light howitzer came up behind us on a slanting bend. It overtook us in the hollow. There was a long stretch of water, which had to be taken at speed. It was a picture of concentrated strength as the three men and six horses took the obstacle. I saw the leading rider in his saddle, and in this peasant boy's face I felt I was watching a team go over a field. There was the same love, the same quiet patience, with which generations of peasants had cut their furrow in snow and rain, sun and wind—straight, disciplined, undeflected. He spoke the same language which his forefathers had used to their animals, he held the reins with the same peasant's fist and showed that same equanimity in enduring hunger and thirst and every face of the elements. Only it is a different plough, and a different seed, which these young steel-helmeted peasants are driving into the future.

The dugouts are nine feet deep. You enter them by narrow shafts and steep steps. They have four to six layers of logs for a ceiling, and they are spacious inside. You can see there's been no economising on material or labour. Our own is the smallest, and there are only four of us. It's a blockhouse which has been taken to pieces and reconstructed underground. There are three layers of logs below the earth covering, a deep shaft down to the window, and a wooden floor. The bunks and walls are made of light, planed wood. It looks very friendly. A shelf, a table, chairs and stools complete the fittings.

The guns are positioned in vegetable gardens between the rows of houses. Their sound breaks against the ruins and what remains of the decrepit huts. Camouflage from the air presents no difficulties; we'll be hard to find. We're not badly off. If they let us stay in these dugouts, we'll survive the second winter all right.

The cobbler built us a stove yesterday. The wheelwright helped him. You should have seen them, the two old boys. The cobbler was so in love with his handiwork that he couldn't tear himself away. He measured and set each brick, explaining everything while smearing the loam in the cracks. His worn hands moulded the edges tenderly, and he murmured "tam" and "tam" and "so" and "so" with every brick he put into place, as if he were casting a spell. He gave of his best. You could see it. Was it right like this? Was it wide enough and high enough? Yes? He would put a piece of sheet-iron underneath, it would be better. Was the door all right? And the stove-pipe? His apple-cheeked face with its child's eyes bent eagerly over the cavity which grew

113

solidly out of the brick and loam. Marussia had to call him three times before he would go for his dinner.

And then the pipe sections. That wasn't at all easy. It had to be properly discussed. The pair of them got quite heated, the cobbler with his high voice, and the toothless wheelwright with his grumbling bass. But then they snorted together, moved the earth, and dug in the pipe.

We have a little frying-pan. It's all the equipment there is for the supplementary cuisine of the dugout. Otherwise Dola and Marussia bring us steaming potatoes and set them down on the table in a wash-basin, which is much simpler. Their mother scrubbed out the dugout this morning. She went at the dirt with a will; believe it or not, she didn't even forget the chair legs. Not that all the dirt on the legs disappeared. Its sticks determinedly. But it's feasible that by the time Christmas comes round it will have succumbed to the repeated attacks.

When she had finished she asked if we'd like a tablecloth, and proudly produced a piece of wallpaper. It is certainly elegant. It's no longer quite new, but the back is still white. I brushed off a starved bug. Now it's impeccable.

In the meantime the *sauna* has started up. It's in the middle of the firing position, forty paces from our dugout. I limped there a little while ago. It's really only a wash-house, but it's very warm and light. The water steams in the copper, and a proper de-lousing chamber will soon rid us of our little partisans.

Russia is a clean country, after all. Very clean! There were two women by the door, each carrying a pair of buckets on a wooden yoke. They asked in a friendly manner: "Comrade wash?" They were going to follow me in, just like that.

Which reminds me of the story of the traveller in Russia: "Russia is the cleanest country in the world. You arrive at Moscow station, and at once a girl comes up and asks you 'Bath, sir?' If you say yes, they're very nice to you. They wash your back and rub your chest; and when you come out there's already another one waiting: 'Bath, sir?' Indeed, Russia is the cleanest country in the world." But we declined the offer: *germanski nix kultura*.

Mild October days. There has been a great deal of rain, but now the days are filled with pale sunlight and the breath of an Indian summer. At night when the moon rises above the far-stretched cloud-banks, its light is reflected by the moist walls of ruins and slanting roofs. Noise carries far, and when you stand at night by the dark barrels of the guns you feel you can touch the front with both hands. And yet its voice hardly penetrates the quiet of my dugout, where I'm mostly living by myself now. The others are on leave or beyond the Volga. There's a lot of building going on at the moment.

What it means to me, this solitude! I can spread myself over the table with books and writing material. I can move about as I like, without having to consider anybody. I have no need to be polite, I don't have to listen to anyone, or to close my ears against conversation. What bliss! I like so much to be alone. I can't bury myself deep enough. There can't be too much of it, this quietness.

I tell myself I have only to pull myself together and find a few kind words and I can make somebody happy. I can give something worth more than anything else in these times, a little love and warmth. That is all we need, because things are not easy for any of us and it does us good sometimes to feel the touch of a hand. We live through love. A few kind words—sometimes it's difficult. It's difficult because words are weak things when we no longer know what to do; difficult because we can't relieve you of anxiety about us. An anxious doubt hangs over every letter, no matter how brave it is. I can feel it growing. But what can I do? I can only stretch out my hands and say once again: Look, I'm here, I'm smiling and I'm quite close to you. Do you feel my confidence? Even if my voice is a few days old, I still live for you in this hour as you live for me. I'm still there, Mother, quite close to you, if you hold still for a moment. Don't you feel it?

Marussia brought a letter. It's a bit strange, when you come to think of it, in a gun position. The little girl was curious. I had to open it right away. But it was written on a typewriter—she couldn't understand that at all. Everything by machine in Germany. Funny country. Can't your father write by hand?—I had to laugh so much. How could I explain it? My knowledge of Russian isn't good enough yet. I sit and sweat over the Russian alphabet and those awful hissing sounds, the *sh*, and *tsh* and *shtsh*. Sometimes she sits by my side and I am the pupil.

I went for a short walk on this glorious October morning. A very short walk. I was like a convalescent, with no other aim than to see and absorb, and enjoy the fact of being there. I walked through the suburb down the decaying street to the Volga, whose bank is dotted with dugouts and beyond which the front line is not far distant. I met the women with yokes carrying pails, in which they bring water up from the river. There are only a few wells here. Before, they had a butt and a pony and trap. Now they fetch the water in buckets, and they float a cabbage leaf on it to stop it slopping over. There was never a water-pipe, of course. I quite forgot to mention that. It's such a crazy idea; only a foreigner would think of it.

In one place soldiers were pulling down a house. The roof collapsed and the moss-covered wooden slates slid down to the ground. There was a whirl of dust, the tumbling of rafters. It was quick work. But there wasn't much of the house before they started. The front had been ripped open and some pieces of fabric were hanging in the wind. Only the Dutch oven was still standing, in all its white glory. Now it stands cold and alone beneath the sky.

How a town changes when the front grips it! What a totally different landscape it presents! Beams, planks, rubble and wire, forlorn household objects, craters and trenches. You stalk across it. It's like a ghost, even in the sunshine. Life has been frightened back into holes and cellars, into the basements whose windows are nailed up with wooden boards and sheet-iron. Sometimes there's a little piece of window-pane left, letting a feeble ray of light into the musty twilight. And yet they stay on, the old men, the women and the children. They are tough. Shy, weary, good-natured, brazen—it all depends. An old man steps aside, mumbles, touches his cap with downcast eyes: the path through the muck of the road is only narrow. A small girl goes to the river, the red scarf on her head shining like a poppy. An old man is packing straw round his hut, because it will be cold soon. How simple! Some boards, one or two logs, and there's an outer wall. In between goes the straw. He drags it up in his tattered sack, heaven knows where from. You build a second stove in winter, and when summer comes you rip it out again. If there's a door missing, you take wood and a hatchet. You do everything with that, joints and all, and its lasts. You don't need a nail or a carpenter, only the hatchet and some wood. This amazing manual skill exists side by side with the remains of the factories.

Over it all tower the green cupolas and the slender spires of the churches, white, shining, neglected, broken. How does it all fit together? Undeveloped, chaotic, inscrutable people.

There's the old man with metal-rimmed spectacles and well-groomed beard, from whose clean room the samovar gleams cheerfully. There's my washerwoman, who has sent her elder boy to Germany and has only his small brother to feed now. She won't give out her washing until it's been ironed. She has mended my foot-rags and a pair of pants, though I didn't even ask her. The little boy is modest and friendly. Then there's the boy who buried his mother, in the garden behind the house, as one buries an animal. He stamped down the earth without saying a word: not a tear, not a cross, not a stone. There's the priest's wife, almost blind from crying. Her husband has been deported to Kazakstan. There are three sons somewhere, God alone knows where. Their photographs show intelligent heads.—Where is the key to all this? It's not just a question of creating order here. A world has collapsed, and the natural order of things was broken up long ago.

CHAPTER X

NORTH OF THE VOLGA

WE walked down to the river, crossed it by the flat wooden bridge, and continued for a while along the road on the other side. Then we took the path up the steep slope. We stopped and looked back. There was a fine rain. Of the iron bridge in the centre of the town[1] there was only one arch left standing. The second had been replaced by a much-propped-up wooden construction. There's a barrier of logs upstream to guard the bridge from floating mines. Here the Volga is still shallow and not very wide—about the same as the Main at Bamberg. On both sides dugouts were hunched against the banks. There were yawning tunnels like mine-openings, paths and steps connecting small gun platforms, and anti-aircraft guns on hill-tops and salients. Digging and burrowing was still in progress everywhere. The noise of gunfire rolled and re-echoed through the valley. Shots sounded from somewhere in the maze of streets and ruins which provide this town's defenders with a thousand-fold ambush. We went on.

There was the dead square, and beyond that the church with the broken cupola from which a street led away towards the enemy. There was no life there. Not even a cat walking hungry over the mounds of rubble. Tall ruins overtowered mountains of broken stone, there were skeletons of houses with caverns for windows, scarcely a roof. The destruction was indescribable. Torn open, pulverised and broken, flattened, convulsed, strewn far and wide, with crater upon crater—how can I describe it. The ground covered with shell cases, respirators and fragments; cables and wire, corrugated iron, poles, twisted girders and torn wire

[1] Kalinin, which the Germans had retaken.

118

aprons blocking the road. Somewhere the tanks were waiting behind cover, ready to break out from the ambush when they were needed. Somewhere else a crowd of people were going down to a stronghold deep in the earth past the Red Cross which stood out by the entrance. Somewhere our hidden trail ran forward through the churned-up gardens.

We slid through a narrow hole into the few remaining rooms of the house which were still not open to the wind. The concrete ceiling was sagging under the weight of debris. A part of the cellar had been partitioned off with double walls. Two doors swung shut behind us, and we were in our den. How comforting a cellar can be! A third bed stood against the wall beneath a map of Europe, a school-map, stretching from Spain to the Urals. I've seen you before, I thought; I know that green of the low countries, the deepening brown of the mountains, the blue ribbons of rivers. You look remarkably like one of the school-maps of Messrs. Justus Perthes of Gotha.—Long-forgotten days came back to me.

There are passage-ways in the cellars and holes between the walls. There are hatches through which you can slip out and go round the pile of rubble to the next opening. There are some staircases which rise like chimneys in the skeletons of the outer walls. Climb one and at every landing you get a better view of the deepening abyss. Here and there a radiator is still hanging over the chasm, otherwise there is nothing to remind you that people once lived there. Sometimes the ruin looks so frail that you hardly dare to cough. This is the area where we operate.

At dusk I went a few hundred yards to the flank to connect a line. I slipped into a deep pit and had to climb the slippery slope again. I groped my way back in the ink-black, rain-swept night, and I don't mind confessing it wasn't easy. I fell into craters, stumbled into runnels and caught myself in wires and fences. My way was paved with loose stones and squelching mud, I crashed into heavy obstacles and trod on treacherous hoops.

The only time I could see the trail was when a flare went up; it was merely a ridge between craters, but I would leap forward.

At last I found the hole again, the hidden light from behind the boarded window—and there was the friendly den. Now it seems twice as cosy. The stove natters and hums, the sparks fly up the chimney. We have made tea in a pail and roasted potatoes in a frying-pan we found. We have rolled ourselves cigarettes or contentedly stuck our pipes between our teeth. What more could one want?

I have taken over an artillery liaison section, and Headquarters Battery has given me old Franz Wolf as wireless operator. It was brilliant sunshine as we went over to the den, where I was last time acting as advanced observer.

The snow had covered the desolation, turning the craters into gentle hollows where you could sink in up to your chest. In the evening the moon hung silver above the mist which veiled the rigid landscape: a few bursts of machine-gun fire, a few flares, sector all quiet.

Last night the temperature dropped from thirty-three degrees Fahrenheit to minus two. We are sitting behind the double doors of our dugout on the side of the slope. There's a quilt hanging between the two doors. The brick stove is as tall as a man, and when it's fired properly, Franz on the top bunk breaks out in a sweat. We only feed it morning and night, then the pipe is closed on the outside with a tin and the loam-and-brick structure radiates its heat hour after hour.

I went along the supply trench which runs forward through the position. It's well made. You can walk upright, but here and there signs warn you of snipers. They lie in wait for each other. Where the supply trench leads into the firing trench it's as well to be quiet. But the companies get their rations by daylight, the sentries keep watch with trench periscopes, and the machine-gun posts have been camouflaged with a snow wall which can be pushed over at any time. Everyone up in the line is wearing the new winter outfit. It's a typically German affair with reversible trousers and jacket, field-grey and white. It has so many pockets, cords and buttons that it takes a while to find one's way about. With it go felt boots, over-gloves, woollen helmets and hoods. Now we're proof against pretty well everything.

It's getting towards midday. The sentries are standing at the parapet or looking silently at the shimmering white of no-man's-land, this tortured, treacherous, wire-infested, mine-infested tract of country, whose features have been named after the wrecks of tanks.

A little while ago a group of men appeared in the trench. The leading one stopped at the first sentry. He was wearing the winter outfit like everyone else. His face was covered with the woollen cap and steel helmet. "You probably don't know me," he said, "I'm your General." The sentry pulled himself smartly to attention and reported everything correct. "Fine, my boy," said the general and produced a piece of chocolate from his pocket. He must have been carrying quite a stock, because no one he met in the trench went empty-handed. "The General's all right," the men are saying.

5th of November, 1942. The night was still. The ice was creaking in the ruts of the roads. Lieutenant Mack and I were going on leave. We walked through the silent town. So long, Kalinin. We took in the picture once more, a last church was glinting in the moonlight and through a gap we saw the shine of the Volga. Then the last huts disappeared and the country opened wide before us. Our words, our breath, were snatched from our mouths by the wind—the eternal breath of the Russian plain.

At five o'clock we were standing by the railway track at a stop marked only by a few goods wagons left stranded by the tide of war. A small group of infanteers were trotting to and fro. It was bitterly cold. At last a trail of smoke appeared, grew taller in the sky and presently came closer. The service train—a couple of coaches, a few goods trucks, a snorting locomotive. We got in and the others made room for us. There wasn't much talk, no sign of relaxation. Twice there were shell-bursts near the track, and the fragments of one hit the coach. The men hardly moved. Vyasma—we changed into the leave train. Smolensk—a break in the journey: night and drifting snow, an icy wind; silent, hurrying figures with awkward luggage; dismal electric light and the sour smell of overcrowded huts.

We went into the town. A visit to the barber, the field book-shop, the cinema and canteen. There was a new recreation room with sturdy square tables and solid chairs. There was music too; it was fine and warm. On the tables were chrysanthemums, living white chrysanthemums. Slowly something thawed inside us and we became strangely lighter at heart. Timidly a little happiness appeared. We started to talk.

Night again, back in the train, rifles piled against the doors, sentries at the end of the corridor, two stoves in each coach. The steam heating alone didn't penetrate. I installed myself on the floor beside the stove. As I lay there half asleep, I felt a companion carefully shifting my feet so that my boots wouldn't catch fire. I have no idea how many people stepped over me during the night.

Vitebsk—Dunaburg, morning and midday. Slowly the face of the landscape was changing. The areas of cultivation grew larger, steppe and scrub retreated, the horizon was bordered by pleasant hills and woods. Herds of cattle again: what a sign of peaceful life! Lithuania brought the first breath of home—a pointed steeple, clean streets, big solid houses. It was Saturday. A steaming *sauna* surrounded by meadows and little gardens. As the train left Dunaburg, somebody started singing: "In der Heimat, in der Heimat, da gibts ein Wiedersehn." It was like a dam bursting.

There are many jokes about the soldier on leave from Russia, about how he marvels at civilisation. It's true. When you come back from the East you find our civilisation so developed, so smooth-running that it seems like a strange machine at first. It's amazing how civilised life is protected from rigour, what a number of comforts we demand as a matter of course.

Those who come back know that nothing exists as a matter of course, yet the transition is easy, because we are too much children of our age not to make use of these things. On the other hand, in such a short time we do not forget that what we are doing is strange. The leave will come to an end, we cannot shake off the thought of our comrades. And so the whole thing has a curious taste. For that reason I find it easy going back. It's more difficult for those who stay behind. For them the waiting must start again, the restlessness, the uncertainty which accentuates their picture of the danger. They cannot see it face to face. One can only know the danger which threatens oneself. That's what gives soldiers their composure—the fact that they can look danger in the eye and gauge its size.

Thus a soldier is differently situated from the women and the fathers whom I saw waiting in the mornings for the postman. Sometimes they would find some small, unobtrusive job to do in the front garden, because they didn't want to show their anxiety. But as for myself, I went back to the front more composed and sure of myself than ever. Life at the front appeared to be clean and straight. How could I have regrets about it? There could be no discussion about that. We have taken up our positions, and conversations are only like signals to show where we stand. Here, too, the soldier's solution is simple. As I once heard an East Prussian say: "Wherever you're put you have to stick it out. That's the way of it."

Pabst returned from leave to find a dramatically changed situation. While he was away, the Red Army had launched a winter counter-offensive, driving the Germans out of Kalinin for the second and last time. The division was falling back on Rzhev, 100 miles south-west.

123

On December the 4th I arrived in P. I covered the last stage of the journey by sledge. The blanket of snow was still a bit shabby in places and you could see the yellow-brown stubble in the fields. On the whole it was a sad sight, this landscape out of which the water-tower of Rzhev was slowly rising. But we had new box-sledges with adjustable runners, and heatable circular tents made of plywood, which could be covered with blocks of snow and used for mobile warfare. The dugouts everywhere looked quite reliable.

Kalinin was evacuated on December the 15th. There can be no question of its having been evacuated for strategic reasons. It was far too important for that. We had to give in before the enemy's assault. The division in whose sector the break-through took place has been disbanded in the meantime. Its remaining men have been divided up among other divisions. The retreat was carried out in reasonable order, but it meant blowing up clothing and food depots, and destroying surgical instruments and other medical supplies. They got out the wounded.

The confusion during the first days of the retreat must have been pretty bad. Our unit lost its way three times during the first night. Vehicles which got stuck were destroyed, generally with their entire loads. Our divisional signals section has only twenty-five per cent of its motor transport left. I found the unit again on December the 25th, about seventy-five kilometres south of Kalinin. They had taken up positions there three days before. The line was to be held. The enemy had followed up with Siberian ski battalions and Cossack squadrons, so that the infantry never managed to disengage themselves. But the enemy didn't find any solid billets; we had burned down everything. All the same, on December the 29th it wasn't only mortars and light artillery which bombarded our sector; they had already brought up Stalin organs as well.

At the time Franz was on artillery liaison duty far forward in a village. The enemy attacked the village fourteen times on the night of the thirtieth. There was no more sleep. Z. had frost-bitten feet. On the thirty-first our new Regimental Commander came up to the village and said: "Well, lads, build yourselves some dugouts, draw some explosives and dig in. . . ." A quarter of an hour later the order came to dismantle and rejoin the unit immediately. When they arrived at our village seven kilometres further on, our vehicles were loaded and everybody was ready to move off. The first houses were already on fire from Russian shells.

When we left the village a little later, the sparks were raining down. The night was red, the columns moved through the snow. It was bitterly cold and the air completely still. The burning villages stood round us in a wide circle—a terrible and beautiful sight, breathtaking in splendour and horror at the same time. With my own hands I threw burning brands into sheds and barns beside the road. Then I rode after the unit together with my companion.

That night we retreated twenty-three kilometres and on the 1st of January twenty more. Men of our reconnaissance battalion, which arrived at six o'clock on New Year's morning, told us they had lost forty dead since leaving K. In K. one of the three battalions of the regiment had been dissolved to provide replacements for the other two. The battalion to which I was attached for so long in K. had been made up to strength on October the 2nd. Now, on December the 31st, it was one hundred and twenty men.

On the last day of the old year Major Christoph left us to take over another section. Looking back, I remember that when he took us over twelve months before, it was like a relief. In the months of hard fighting which followed he became the focus of the section. The more difficult the situation, the greater was the confidence he inspired. He could be severe, yet when it seemed that things had reached their limit, his severity turned to kindness. He would come out with little words of encouragement, giving everyone his task; then everything would be all right. He was a born leader. He would arrive without warning, no word of the bush telegraph preceded him. He was at home everywhere. For all his strict discipline, when his tall, heavy figure appeared on a gun-site, everyone would discover a kind of light-heartedness. He would appear at a new look-out on the second day at the latest. When he left us, the heavy howitzers sang him a farewell serenade. He must have read all the respect, love and devotion in the eyes of his men, for everybody loved him.

At 1500 hours it is dark, at 1700 it is deep night. When an eight-man patrol and a patrol from the next-door company swung themselves over the parapet of the trench, they were quickly lost in the liquid whiteness of no-man's-land. There was just the heavy creak of snow, barely overlaid by bursts of fire from our machine-guns, and they were gliding through the gap in the wire. It was completely quiet for a moment. Thirty yards away they were lying close to the enemy's trench. We could see the dark embrasure of the machine-gun post where the patrol was to break in. Tensely we waited for the outcome.

Had the enemy noticed anything? No?—How long seconds could be! Then everything happened quickly: some shadows jerking forward, a rapid movement, a dull thump in the trench, suddenly the first burst from a machine-pistol.

One of our own? Or one of the enemy's?—It must have been ours, it was the zipping sound.

There were the dull explosions of some hand-grenades, a second burst from the machine-pistol—then one man came back: the patrol leader. He swayed, collapsing in the trench: "Fire! Give them covering fire! They've got it all to themselves!"

But there was no need to bring down the heavy stuff. The men did the job themselves. They didn't dream of retiring. Exactly according to plan, they completed their mission, half of them bombing from the parapet, half of them in the trench itself. The enemy tried to cut them off. From communication trenches the

Russians crept up—four—six—eight men of them—approaching from every side. But the patrol went on throwing their grenades, keeping the enemy at bay. They blew up a couple of machine-gun posts with concentrated charges, but after that they lost their overall view of the enemy's trench system. A sergeant-major ran after them and brought them back. On the way they threw a Teller-mine into the machine-gun post nearest to our trench. Total bag: three machine-gun posts and eighteen of the enemy.

"Clear the trench! Everybody back to their dugouts!" shouted the Company Commander. But it was another half-hour before the enemy began some haphazard harassing fire, and even that was given up after a while. Ivan must have had quite a shock. The other company's patrol got five of his men at the same time.

Through the entrance of the dugout man after man came hesitatingly in. At last they were together again—the whole patrol. They wanted to see what had happened to the patrol leader: "Is it bad?"—"Damn them," grated the Sergeant. "Just wait, in four weeks I'll be back again; then I'll settle up with them, the bastards! I know their trench now."

10th of January, 1943. "Schnapps essential, sugar an advantage, water optional." From the time-honoured recipe plus a few lemons, we brewed some grog. A guitar and an accordion provided the music, which we relayed by line to the neighbouring dugouts. Afterwards the company asked for the band for a birthday celebration. We tucked our instruments under our arms and walked through the moonlit trench.

How quiet it was suddenly between the two islands of gaiety. The figure of my companion bent and slithered through the winding trench enclosed by high, pale walls of shimmering white. Our steps were muted by the loose snow, and the frost made a thick coating round cables and branches.

The quiet on our sector leaves a bitter taste in our mouths: the boys at Stalingrad are making a tough stand. In the morning we had a little disturbance. Ivan took exception to the smoke going up from our dugouts. Grenkowitz threw a doubtful look towards the ceiling, and Franz, who had just set out on his morning walk, came hopping back, swearing. He had been blown head first into the waste pit.

In the course of all this we enjoyed a little joke. A few hand-grenades landed on the dugout of the doctor as he was peacefully reading a book. The covering noise was deceptively genuine, and the blackened marks on the fresh snow looked absolutely authentic.

Slowly I'm compiling a new account of all this, sentence by sentence and word by word. It takes its form from many notes and a first draft. But I miss the quietness with which to sur-round myself within these four walls and so to give it my un-divided attention.

Today we talked about what was going on inside ourselves, trying to take stock of our feelings. We recalled a lot of things, especially last winter. Our conclusions weren't very subtle. Sensitivity is no longer our strong suit. We do things without hesitation which we wouldn't have dreamed of at one time. Should it ever occur to us that one might shrink from doing them, we would treat it as a joke. And sights which would once have shaken us deeply, we now view with scientific detachment.

Franz said that on his leave he once started to talk about the retreat from Kalinin. It was amongst men. But they looked at him so oddly that he saw how impossible it was and said no more. He talked to us about his grandmother, whose mother used to talk about the war of 1870; the horror of it was still alive a generation afterwards. We talked about the "bloody" battles of Gravelotte and Mars la Tour, and then the Great War and the chaos which followed, the revolution and the formation of new fields of power. We tried once more to understand our own time—the end of a phase of history, the grotesque masquerade in which a world is falling in ruins.

On November 19th the Russians had sprung the trap at Stalingrad. An attempt to relieve von Paulus from the South-West had been frustrated. Now, in January, the encircled Sixth Army of 200,000 men was facing the greatest disaster in German military history. At the same time orders had been given for the withdrawal of the Caucasus armies. Von Kleist recrossed the Don, covered by an improvised army group under von Manstein.

CHAPTER XI

THE RZHEV BRIDGEHEAD

THE thermometer has fallen to forty-five degrees below freezing. The snow is sparkling and blowing about in fine crystals. Each step throws it up, it glitters in the sun and refracts the evening light. At night it glitters blue beneath the moon, which makes the landscape more rigid than ever. A little while ago I came back from the look-out to my dugout, with the snow screaming beneath my skis. The forced intake of breath hurt my lungs, and my eyelashes were thickly covered with ice. The sledges on the road could be heard for miles in the windless night.

How good it was to enter the warm dugout with its circle of friendly light! The snow showered from my woollen helmet as I tore it off. Grenkowitz peeled off my over-jacket. Since the day we arrived he has taken over all the duties of a housewife, washing up the dishes, sweeping out the room, looking after the stores. If somebody wants to pour out the coffee for himself, Grenkowitz feels hurt. He has his little peculiarities. But then, who hasn't? We have to take each other as we are, and if ever it's impossible, we say so. This way we have created an island of peace in the middle of war, where comradeship comes easily and there's always somebody to laugh. I often take up my guitar. Henning has sent me the *Kilometerstein*, a song-book with a lot of long-forgotten tunes.

At night we go through the old soldiers' songs, both the hearty and the sentimental ones, the ironical ones and the lusty. And whenever things get a bit much, we sing.

Yesterday evening I sat over a letter. It wasn't a proper letter, just a scrap of paper which had come from far away, across a great waste of bitterness and silence. It has affected me more than I can say. There are moments when we are helpless, when we are deprived of all strength of will. At such moments our heart makes foolish jumps. Then we pass a hand over our eyes and slam the door shut, because we have to force ourselves in a direction in which we don't want to go.

But in fact the heart goes its own ways, and we listen to the sound behind the door, knowing full well that there lies everything which gives sense to our living. Thus we are chastised like Don Quixote, and pain makes us our true selves.

How widely opinions differ about the future shape of the world. The differences are not only vertical between nations, but also horizontal between factions as they prepare for another battle alongside the battle of arms. Many of our enemies now see the need to win the peace after the war. It's a relief out here to be away from the hatred and blind passions, the cowardice and the dirt. War demands a man's whole being. Arms speak unequivocally, beyond the reach of wishful thinking.

There are about fifty-four degrees of frost. The snow blows round the ruins and collects in the shattered houses. Ceaselessly nature wipes over everything. Not a trace remains, not a footprint or shell crater.

The landscape grows into the town, and the houses are only stage-sets beyond the muzzles of our guns. The narrow path runs like a ribbon down the shining surface of the wide street. At night I follow it in the shivering moonlight and beneath the pale-blue arcs of the flares. Then I fork off down the steep slope of the gully and up again to the dugout on the far side.

25th of January, 1943. 0645. All three of us woke up with a start. A bombardment. So they're attacking after all. The question is what are they after. We try to gauge the calibre of the guns and the weight of the shelling. The sound is familiar. Our movements are businesslike, the atmosphere tense and happy. We sniff outside like hunters smelling their game. The telephone starts, hurried messages and questions, which show how excited we are. "Attack against company on the right."—"Enemy in the trench of the company beyond."—"Rear-link gone, all lines cut." Switch to wireless. The infantry guns retaliate. Soon the regiment is bombarding Zones 12 and 13. Trajectories criss-cross above us.

0730. The enemy's support waves get pinned down in the barrage. The attack on two further companies to the right was repelled, partly in hand-to-hand fighting. The penetration has been sealed off and a tank attack from the left was brought to a standstill. Reserves are coming up, and a line patrol goes back through the fire of the enemy, which is gradually slackening. The gully behind the firing position is straddled by bands of blackened snow, two hundred yards across. The snow looks as if it had been burnt ; the way is barred by rocks and lumps of earth.

0915. In the middle of the trench taken by the enemy a group of our men are still holding out. Our snipers have taken over the supply trench between battalion headquarters and the company on the right. They shoot every Russian who escapes from the barrage or tries to retreat. Our forward observer there is having a field-day, firing the guns for all they're worth. The enemy is stuck. His rocket launchers are firing into the sector senselessly.

1010. The enemy keeps trying to push on. But the telephone lines have long been restored, and the regiment has every single battery on the line. It's a pleasure to listen to the fire control. On the infantry line they're already getting music again. Jochen Grenkowitz has just come back from line patrol ; there were six breaks this side of the bridge alone. "Just think of it," he said, "I was mending the line, lying flat as a pancake, when a company runner passed by. 'Hi, Jochen, having a good time?'—'Wait a minute,' I said, 'where are you going?'—'Me? to the cinema!' and God damn it, he went off into the town."

Towards midday the sun was shining, and the trench was in our hands again. The counter-attack didn't meet much resistance. The encircled party held out the whole time. Our losses were astonishingly small. A Volga German deserter said that of the three hundred Russians who stormed the trench, two hundred had already been killed when he deserted. The rest fell to the snipers and grenades, and the supporting wave went down under the shelling. Between our own trench and the enemy's wire we can count five hundred and fifty dead. The booty amounts to eight heavy and twelve light machine-guns, thirty machine-pistols, five flame-throwers, four anti-tank rifles and eighty-five rifles. It was a Russian penal battalion of fourteen hundred men. They won't form up against us again.

At 2030 fifteen columns, each consisting of about thirteen men with sledges and equipment, were reported turning into the wood to our front. At 2045 there were forty or fifty men more. Shells went howling into the wood from the whole regiment. The ricochets of the heavy section made an infernal noise, bursting fifteen feet above the ground. Our own made their deep organ sound, rushing and rattling in the icy air. This party of Russians didn't worry us again either.

There's a singing, happy silence in the sector. The skies are gloriously blue, tension is slackening off. Ivan hasn't come our way again. The snow in the air drifts blackish-brown in the sunlight, with many gleams of white. Our spotter plane is still overhead, glinting and sparkling as it turns to finish off one enemy battery after another. It's nearly midday. Seven Russian guns have been silenced already.

The day before yesterday? That's a long time ago. The dead will soon be covered with snow if Ivan doesn't come to collect them. That's something he's just started to do for the first time in our experience. He incurs yet further losses in the process. We heard the communique and commentary which mentioned our doings here. But otherwise we have been talking about Stalingrad.[1] There isn't much to say. We have known for a long time what's going on there. But we also know that the Russian reserves aren't inexhaustible; they're bleeding to death with inexorable certainty.

We can compare the casualties. We count the dead, and there's no cheating. We only count the dead we can see. Our total losses of two days ago didn't reach a tenth of the number of enemy corpses which are still lying in no-man's-land. The conclusion is inescapable.

The wind is still howling, shrilly and plaintively. At certain bends in the trench it whips up shivering columns of snow dust. When we stick our heads above the parapet, it stings our faces. Over our dugout steps the snow has broken in like a moving dune more than six feet high.

But the wind is blowing towards the enemy's embrasures, driving the snow into his sentries' eyes. It's all to the good. Ten Company is doing a patrol tonight.

Lieutenant Camp is happy. His voice over the telephone sounded clear and gay. Congratulations are pouring in for the Tenth over every line. The patrol came back without losses. They rolled up three hundred and fifty yards of trench, blew up five dugouts and six machine-gun posts, took two prisoners, two anti-tank rifles, two machine-pistols, and ten rifles, including four automatics. They beat off two counter-attacks in hand-to-hand fighting and only broke off when their ammunition ran short. Coming back, they knocked out a camouflaged dugout with twelve men inside. The enemy had thirty-nine dead. The infantry-artillery co-operation went like clockwork. A thing like that bucks you up. "Very good, Camp, very good," said Colonel Zickwolff. "Tomorrow you can hand in the names of your men for decoration." The whole regiment was pleased. We too can use a snow-storm as an ally.

[1] Von Paulus surrendered on 31st of January.

7th of February, 1943. A forty-five-mile-per-hour wind is whipping along the snow. It chases in great sheets under the low-flying clouds. Sky and earth converge in a great bluster. Visibility is four hundred yards. The daylight passes quickly. I fought my way against the wind to the *sauna*. The sentries on the bridge had withdrawn to a sheltered spot, where they stood silent and awkward-looking in their furs and straw-overshoes. On the slopes leading down to the Volga two carefree figures were ski-ing. Otherwise I met nobody but some solitary figures who appeared and vanished like snow-clouds; they passed by without a look or a greeting, intent only on reaching their destination. When I came back, the entrance to the dugout was completely covered over again. I slid down in an avalanche. Between the two doors the snow had formed a mat. It nestled in every crack and in the folds of the quilt, and fell into my collar as I lifted up the curtain to slip underneath.

Now a glorious day again.

The wind has veered to the East and there are twenty-two degrees of frost. I came back from the look-out and read until the light became too feeble. Then I put the book aside and watched Grenkowitz standing in front of the stove. His face was lit by the fire, and there was an atmosphere of smoke and toasted bread. Franz was sitting on his bunk, dangling his legs. The outlines became vague, the colours pale. We didn't speak. There was only the sound of our movements in the room and the light which came from the stove and the slowly darkening window. *L'heure bleue.* So strange and unreal, this time between the day that has passed and the day that's to come.

When Grenkowitz lit the candle in the corner by the stove, it was already evening. The friendly crockery looked down from the shelf. The white cups, the gold-trimmed saucers, the little plates with flower patterns. How ugly it all looked when we fished it out of the ruins. And now how bright it is, the wall by the stove, the cheerful cover on the bed, the friendly ceiling with its white paper and dark-red beams. I thought of it all as Grenkowitz placed the candle on the table, laying the crockery, putting the butter and meat carefully on a plate and neatly piling the slices of bread.

Then even Franz made an effort and plunged from his silence into reality. He grumbled. Was that all the meat there was? "Yes," said Grenko, "and quite enough too. There wasn't any more to be got." He gave a slight grin out of the corner of his mouth, just as he does when he has a good hand at poker. Grenko looks after our rations and has the delightful habit of cheating us for our own benefit. He builds up secret reserves and produces them at breakfast. He keeps back the precious sugar from our coffee, so as to surprise us at tea-time, when the good tea would otherwise be ruined by saccharine. In short, he's the born housewife. And whenever he has played his little deception on us, he beams all over his face.

But this time Franz wasn't easily appeased. Something must have soured his humour. After dinner he exploded; he suddenly reached for his cup, weighed it in his hand, and threw a searching glance towards the corner by the stove. "Look," he said, "a mouse!"—"Heavens, not with our best china!" breathed Grenkowitz, reaching behind him and pressing a rifle into Franz's hand.

"Come out, my little fellow," Franz murmured, cocking the rifle while his eyes pierced the darkness. Then there was a loud bang, a flash and the smell of powder. The mouse lay on the boards, shot clean through the head. It's a rough way of doing things, but we don't have a mouse-trap.

The other day the Divisional Chaplain paid us a visit. The meal was interrupted in a similar manner. He confessed afterwards that when he came in he had wondered why we had a pistol lying on the table during dinner; he had taken us for a rather war-like lot. He found the method quite good, but his ears still hurt him half an hour afterwards. Very regrettable.

Following the fall of Stalingrad, the Russians launched an offensive westward from Voronezh and on 7th of February retook Kursk. Kharkov fell eight days later, leaving von Manstein and von Kleist in imminent danger of being cut off. At the same time Hitler at last accepted professional advice that the forward position before Moscow was untenable. Orders were given for the troops there to be withdrawn to a closer, straighter line covering Smolensk.

I spent the day saying good-bye to my books. My time was divided between the *Conversations* of Frederick the Great and Henri de Catt, and *Little Impressions of Paris* by Pierre Champion, de son Vieux Quartier. I found a few sentences I liked very much: "One would have to be a terrible barbarian, my dear sir, to put down some poor devils who, after all, got into our quarrels quite against their will." Or: "Cherish your sensibility! It's one of nature's finest gifts. Even if it exposes us to many complications, it is the source of many pleasures if tempered with commonsense."

Total war may have obliterated the distinction between soldiers and civilians, but it will always be regarded as dishonourable to use weapons against women and children. And among honourable nations there will always be obedience to the conventions which govern the fate of prisoners of war. You can do your duty without forgetting yourself, and you have to keep at a distance from things if you're to see them in the right perspective.

The post brought me a parcel from Jo with some samples of Quimper pottery. He, like myself, loves its coarse exuberance and strong colours. They look strangely gay in this Eastern world, and they fill me with sadness, because they recall the richness of that life of ours whose memory is buried deeper with each succeeding year. One has to fight against drying up and resigning oneself. A vessel which stands too long in an arid atmosphere begins to show cracks. So I will stow the things in my pack when we move, because that's what we're going to do. We are moving out of our dugouts into the snow. We're going to shorten the front-line. Because that's the sensible thing. Because it's good that something should happen. Because a little bit more or less does not matter in this country.

We have sat here long enough in the Rzhev bridgehead. We got to know it well, this town, with its geometrical streets, the ruins of churches, the three bridges across the Volga with its steep slopes, the gorges, the ruined stone buildings where our observers are sitting on the north bank.

From there, you had a wide view over the enemy's positions across the trenches and snow parapets. You could see as far as the hills where villages had once been—now only to be guessed at from the lonely lines of tall trees beyond the range of our guns. Our trenches ran at the foot of the Bastion. In front of them lay the wrecks of tanks. All this has been stamped on our memory. It became part of our lives because willy-nilly we had to live with it.

Adieu Rzhev, city of ropemakers and churches! There isn't much left of you. We're leaving you without a fight, but the enemy will remember that he didn't prise this stone from our rampart by his own exertions.

We are blowing up the railway. We are laying low the towers. We won't leave you with a single round, not even with any labour, because your women and children prefer to come with us. When the bridge goes up, which once carried the trains on their way to Staritza, that will be the signal. But you won't know it. Soon there'll be only Sergeant-Major Jakobs and his men left north of the Volga.

17th of February, 1943. We have heard the communiqué. I can't deny that it filled us with a kind of bitter scorn. They talk about desperate battles in Kharkov, where fifteen tanks were knocked out. If that was the whole defence of Kharkov, it was pathetic. They might as well pack up down there. An army which gets a constant licking isn't much good any more. I'm sorry, that's the way I feel. Perhaps we do them an injustice. But if it's true, as we think, that it's the SS—the *Grossdeutschland*,

Reich and *Adolf Hitler* divisions—then we understand it only too well. It's not the young troops, not the mercenaries, not the celebrated assault divisions on which you can rely. It's the old ones, the burnt-out ones, who'll stand their ground. At least, it's significant that the troops have always stayed put up there on Lake Ladoga and Lake Ilmen, and in their mud-holes on the Volchov.[1] And, as far as I know, they're not SS units. You can see those in the newsreels, which is something we don't stoop to.

One day our battalion shot up eighteen tanks before Beshenki. At Martinovo there were twenty knocked out on a front of three hundred yards. In the woods before Tabrakovo they had to decide by rota who was allowed to take on the next, because in the beginning they all ran after them—the major, the adjutant and the duty officer—leaving the command post deserted. Even the sergeant of the anti-tank gun left his weapon and joined in the hunt with a limpet mine. And the tanks came day after day. Day after day the companies got smaller. It went on day and night, and hour after hour. But our Bavarians fought to the death. In these battles the artillery regiment lost twenty-five signallers alone, not counting observers.

We have lost a number of people via the casualty clearing station: malaria, rheumatic fever, influenza—heaven knows what. Generally strong lads. It's the old story: strength isn't the main thing. It's the lean old sweats who can keep it up longest. Franz and I enjoy excellent health.—Franz has found a doll for himself. Such things exist. She has a round, Eastern face, sturdy legs and a pretty blue dress. We have christened her Babette. She sits astride my guitar and Franz swears he'll take her to bed with him tonight: rock-a-bye baby. . . .

At 0300 I got an order to go on liaison duty with the infantry in the morning. At half-past nine I was with Colonel Zickwolff, just in time to wish him a happy birthday. He kept me to lunch

---

[1] On the Northern Army Group and Finnish fronts the troops were locked in static warfare most of this time.

and coffee. Meanwhile my men have installed themselves in the dugout which belonged to the commander of the departing section. I must say it's princely, the Villa "Volga View". In the meantime, things had to be organised. Tomorrow another of our famous patrols will go out; we'll have to give the pigeons something to peck at. The evacuation seems to have been postponed. In the West there's gunfire. We aren't worrying. Everything is fine.

Yesterday I was busy from morning till late at night. At dawn an enemy patrol broke into our trench. It cost us one man killed, but the enemy left three dead and a prisoner. According to the prisoner the spot where our patrol was to go this morning was an assembly area. So the patrol was organised as a counter attack. With my old signallers I fought my way forward through a wild storm. The weather was so bad that we couldn't check on fire orders and there was a nasty business with two short rounds. One of them almost got me, the other killed two people in the trench. All the same, the patrol did very well and blew up the assembly area.

I had a lot to do because of the mishap. I was racing between company and battalion, and between Colonel Zickwolff and my Regimental Commander. When at last I got home, I slept for thirteen hours. Today I have dictated a full report about the patrol, brought my diary up to date and had endless telephone calls in the evening because of a bombardment. It's after midnight now and every gun in the regiment is still firing. It's the third such shoot. I'm terribly tired, otherwise I'm fine.

At first light the storm was still blowing and Ivan was in the trench again. It was on Nine Company front six or seven of his men made it out of twenty-five. There was a brief, wild fight, hand-to-hand and knee-to-knee. There was no time to fire, just enough to swing a rifle and club the nearest skull. Within twenty-five minutes the trench was clear again. The enemy left three dead and a prisoner. The prisoner said there were a hundred men lying in reserve in the enemy positions which we call the Starling's Nest and the Dugout Garden. They arrived last night.

We are organising a counter attack. This afternoon we fought our way forward with the wind in our faces. It blew with such force that we could hardly hold ourselves on the narrow, iced-up tracks. Over the parapets went clouds of snow dust. The wire, the tanks, the craters and the ruins by the park disappeared in a flurry of white. The enemy position forty yards from our trench looked like an island in the snowstorm. The gunners checked the range, but even the shells of the Heavies went down without a trace behind the veil of snow. We only heard the roll of explosions from somewhere.

As a result of all this we have had to forgo bombarding the Dugout Garden. The infantry must manage without proper artillery preparation. At 0830 the heavy guns will merely shell the area for one minute. The rest is up to the men of the Ninth. As usual. The last, vital stage is always left to the infantry and nobody can help them when it comes to the point. 0800. They're getting ready. They load the machine-pistols, buckle on their equipment, grab the bags of grenades, and build up steps in the trench with empty ammunition boxes. All the while the observers of the heavy artillery are crouching thirty yards in the rear behind the ruins of a house, and those of the infantry guns are pulling back their fire to twenty-five yards from the trench. Three sergeants and sixteen men press themselves against the parapet ready to jump.

0825 . . . 0829 . . . one more minute . . . thirty seconds . . . the hands of the synchronised watches move towards zero . . . there go the heavy and light howitzers, the infantry guns, the mortars. The fire comes down close to the trench, the black smoke shoots upwards like a wall, and the infantry jump into the last bursts from their own guns. It's a sudden, wild movement, a cat-like jumping through the treacherous snow, a second of deadly, breathless tension, in which all eyes follow the thin line of men racing

141

through no-man's-land in great leaps. With the last shell they're in the enemy's trench.

Like a thunderstorm the patrol is on them, dividing up and running down both sides of the trench. The first dugouts blow up, machine-gun posts erupt, ugly black mushrooms spring up, and the grenades continue the clearing-up, small flat explosions spreading ahead. Through splashing dirt and over collapsing brown figures the patrol fight their way. One charge flies into a dugout without exploding. The enemy stream out and fall one over another into the fire of the machine-pistol. A grenade does the rest.

The men are black in the face. Some are scratched. The heavy artillery is coming down on the edge of the wood. It covers the communication trench, but it can't stop reinforcements coming through. The enemy assemble for counter attacks. Three are repelled, then the patrol disengages itself. The fire of the heavy artillery moves back on the trench. With whistling lungs the men fall back into their own trench. The last is Sergeant-Major Jakobs. They're all back. Blackened, dirt-encrusted, exhausted. A trail of red goes from the trench up to the aid post. But over on the enemy's side, on a front of two hundred and twenty yards, ten dugouts and twenty machine-gun posts have been blown up, eleven heavy machine-guns and a 45 mm. anti-tank gun destroyed. Seventy to ninety dead are lying in the trench. The patrol got right to the heart of the assembly position.

Today it was so warm that we stretched ourselves out in the sun like cats, blinking happily into the light. I put on skis and went across the Volga, falling twice on the steep slope. I came back so glowing and re-charged with solar energy that life started to dance in my blood again.

The snow on the south slope has already melted. The water is pouring in streams over the systems of steps that lead to the dugouts. The one we live in now is a masterpiece. It's a big, roomy rectangle with a partition to shut off the sleeping quarters.

The lower half of the walls has a wainscoating of planed boards, the upper half is covered with light wooden tiles. The ceiling is papered white. The transoms have all been boarded over and are finished with smooth edges. There's a corner seat, a shelf, a square table; it's all very snug.

Since yesterday I have been on artillery liaison and artillery duty with the rear-guard. There is one battalion left on the regimental sector. Today it was fairly quiet until twelve o'clock. Then lively firing on Nine Company sector, the Volga bridge and the southern part of the town. Artillery, mortars, anti-tank guns. Two hundred men were attacking from Dugout Garden. A duel developed. I watched all this from the roof of a large stone build-ing. The enemy broke into our trench. I brought back the barrage another hundred and fifty yards, till it was almost on our own positions. The enemy was thrown back leaving twenty-five to thirty dead and one prisoner.

1430. In Zone 18 Ivan's in the trench. He can't be thrown out any more. We seal off. We have four Light and one 100 mm. gun batteries left for the whole divisional sector. The look-outs are widely dispersed. The points which most concern us are on the flanks and in the centre, in Zone 15, the Dugout Garden. The enemy tries again and again to attack here, but with weak forces. The telephone goes all the time; I drag it with me between the dugout and the look-out, up an enormous broad ladder which stands in the open against the side of a house, then over planks between chimney stacks up to a point at the end of the north wall. There I stand on a second, smaller ladder and look over the parapet.

1730. Two Light batteries pull out; the two others stand behind the first new rear-guard position and fire another thousand rounds till 2100. The companies of the rear-guard disengage from the enemy. The last telephone lines are dismantled. For a short time we go over to wireless. On the left flank the enemy is exploiting his break-through, but the disengagement goes according to plan.

Villa "Volga View" is blown up. Captain Gross and Lieutenant Schubert are still standing alone on the road. We pack up and go back too. Beneath the bridge on the road which leads back from the front, a little group from battalion headquarters stands waiting for the last companies to leave the trenches. Up in the north part of the town the Stalin organ is firing its rockets. The ground already has the atmosphere of no-man's-land, this strange air of excitement and danger in which there are only the vague shapes of fighting men, prowling like foraging wolves. We cross the Volga bridge for the last time.

CHAPTER XII

THE RETREAT ACROSS THE DNIEPER

At regimental headquarters the officers were standing pale and tense round Colonel Zickwolff. Would everything be all right? A hissing carbide lamp threw its cold light round the bare dugout. My task was completed. When I came out, my little group was ready to march off. Off we went. Fyodor the pony stepped forward, the cart began to roll. We turned our backs on the Volga. Black holes yawned in the road, Pioneer sentries stood by the mine fields. Flames were leaping up from a stone building, red in the caverns of the windows, furiously roaring through the roof. The landscape had become bare in the last few days. Our last landmarks, houses and towers, were no longer standing. Explosive charges lay ready beneath whatever remained.

Soon we were on the open road. Before us we could still see the fire of the rear-guard batteries; then they were left behind, guns and limbers at the ready, shadows of men and horses with hanging heads. The road was ice-bound. We stumbled and slipped, walking round dirty, frozen puddles, in which the ice creaked and the water spurted out as Fyodor strained in the shafts. We overtook dark columns. We were marching fast.

In the South an enormous fire threw a pencil of light into the sky like a steeply-inclined searchlight and the snow was coloured with a warm, gentle red. Our necks were cut by a north-east wind blowing powdered snow and torn cloud-shreds before us in the clear, starry night. At 2030 a sheet of lightning flickered behind us, filling the landscape from horizon to horizon. Afterwards came the dull roll of the explosions. It was an unforgettable sight. The Volga bridges, the last towers: now they stood no

145

longer.... Soon the last of our men would be coming back across the ice on the river.

We marched on. Marching all the time. Sometimes we thought of our dugout. We sang, because you have to keep up your spirits somehow. After two hours' rest in an overcrowded billet, we moved on just as the rear-guard battalion was coming in. They had disengaged according to plan. It was only on the right that things didn't seem to be going quite smoothly. The flares went up: the enemy was attacking. But already the assault guns were going back to the front, rattling monsters in the white-swirling night.

When we reached the unit at six in the morning, I could do nothing but warm my hands for half an hour round a mug of hot coffee. I was too tired to eat. Later it got better. I pulled off my boots and noticed that the stocking and rags on my right foot were soaked with blood. I fell asleep. Good morning, good night!

At three next morning we moved off again. Fires were colouring the turquoise sky. How could a barbaric spectacle be so charming, so indescribably beautiful?

At seven o'clock we were ready for action, and I found myself doing artillery liaison with the Brake Grenadier Regiment. I stood behind a snow parapet and watched the marching Russian columns coming up from beyond the little river. I watched them form up in companies and advance on motor-sledges. Then our artillery got on to them.

At 1350 we marched on. From behind a window a woman, who had stayed behind for some reason, showed her child the German soldiers for the last time. There was despair in her eyes. We marched. Night fell. We rested for two hours in crowded houses. We marched on. The snow wind was blowing. The flares went up. When the column stopped, we tried to find shelter from the wind. The riders were lying in front of their horses, their faces flat on the ground, their arms round their rifles, shaggy and shapeless in their furs, looking like bears or Tibetans. We walked along the battery. The fires gave the snow a violet colour. Day-break. We rested for three hours, sleeping for two of them. Then we marched on again. The sun burnt our faces. The snow glistened. Our lips began to crack.

As the sun sank behind the heights on the other side of the great river, we marched into A. It was like a parade, men, horses and carts, smartly in step. In the evening when we sat round the table, we had deep lines in our faces—those typical lines from the corners of the eyes and nose. In the morning the guns were ready for action.

Since the day before yesterday we have been in a new rear-guard position. Despite the strain I'm very well. There's bright sunshine, and a little later I'll be going on with Franz Wolff in our little wireless cart. We don't expect any contact with the enemy before tomorrow.

Just as I was hurriedly finishing my report, there was a fighter attack. It spattered dirt on my paper and blew the window panes into my back. Lieutenant K. was wounded.

In the afternoon I went with Franz Wolff and Jean Braun to act as artillery liaison with the Uhl Battalion. We had our little cart again, with Fyodor as our horse. Jean acted as driver and operator at the same time.

We drove over the hills in brilliant sunshine. Six Russian bombers were approaching, with four of our fighters on their tails. They clamped up on them from below. Before the wild chase disappeared behind the woods, two of the big Russian kites turned over on their sides and crashed trailing sheets of smoke behind them.

We crossed the Dnieper, which here was only as wide as the Kinzig. In N. the infantry went into position, digging and moving about in small groups on a flat stretch of ground in front of the woods where the enemy will emerge. The left flank of the regiment is stuck. Enemy forces have broken through and are already holding the ground. The flank is being strengthened. We are pushing out standing patrols and preparing an attack.

147

8th of March, 1943. The enemy is coming up with five thousand men on the left flank of the division. Our spotters report their movements. Our own attack is already meeting strong resistance. But towards evening all is quiet again. The sun goes down with enchanting colours, spreading a smoky golden sheen which contrasts with the clear blue shadows of the winter night spreading slowly in the east.

The two of us went across the hard snowfields, while Franz took the cart in a wide detour across the bridge. They grew smaller and smaller in the lonely landscape, Fyodor, the cart and Franz on the driver's seat. Then they came up towards us again over the gentle hills.

We found the battery ready to move off. The houses were empty with all those signs of a final departure which make human habitations so sad. We joined the column and marched into the setting sun. Evening came. The road grew hard, the wind biting. It was no longer silver and playful, but blue and hard as steel. It clawed at my face and tore holes in my body. I was cold in my thin coat without a shirt beneath it. I asked for a fur coat and it was a heavy weight on my tired feet. Something was wrong with my left knee; we had done ten kilometres, and there were thirty more to do. Fatigue gripped my head like a stunning, stupefying cap. Finally it was only my feet that went on marching, step after step, awkwardly stumbling against the wind. The last two kilometres were through deep snow, away from the main road. I went as slowly as a very old man. From a gully behind me where the vehicles got stuck, the curses of the drivers rose into the icy night like the cries of damned souls.

It was past midnight. The billets were overcrowded, and miserable, stinking shacks at that. We sat down heavily as if festooned with lead. With heavy eyes we watched the bread toasting on the iron stove and listened to the humming of the samovar. Despite everything we sang. We shared the billet with some Ukrainian partisan-hunters. After a while they got up to make room for us and went out into the night after their quarry.

When it got light we saw a heap of indescribably dirty rags lying on the stove. There were mountains of stinking dirt in the corners. But that's Russia. And it was typical of Russia, too, that from all this muck there crept out a little girl of sweet, angelic beauty. She had big eyes and fair locks, and yet she was destined so quickly to fade, to become like her grandmother, so ugly and dirty and witch-like, that one wouldn't touch her with a glove.

Well, we cleaned out the sty. The Ukrainians helped us, grinning. They pushed out the dirt with shovels and boards. Afterwards the room was habitable.

The day passed quickly. It began early, after three hours sleep. That was because the horses come first, and to find shelter for both horses and men wasn't easy. But in the evening we were singing again, feeling we had done a good day's work and hoping for a good night's rest. When I hung up the guitar and sat on my blanket, the last man awake as usual, enjoying a moment's solitude, a runner came with the order: "You've got to be at . . . by six o'clock at the latest." I looked at the map—ah, well . . . Reveille at 0300, move at 0400. Now its 2200. "Sleep quicker, comrade."

Franz and Jean had something to say when I pulled off their blankets at 0300. Jean clung to his like a child to its mother's breast; he had slept exactly an hour and a half, after doing sentry duty.

The lonely cart creaked along the riverside in the early morning, along narrow paths, through villages where only the sentries were awake, past silent thatched huts where the smoke was not yet rising. When we had to cross the Dnieper, we looked suspiciously at the ice. The cart took it at speed but it broke under the rear wheels. We just managed to reach firm ground. Encouraged by our cries Fyodor took the bank. Then we climbed the hill, from which a view opened up over the river valley.

The river is only young here, but it cuts a wide bed across the broad, undulating plain.

It has put its mark on the landscape, with its steep banks and the deep gorges of its tributaries. It makes a splendid, wild rent through these gentle contours, these shades of brown and white which are formed by the fallow land and the snow fields, the dark waves of the woods, and the pale, wintry skeletons of brushwood on the wide circle of the horizon.

We enjoyed this view as we trekked along the steep slope and over the plateau, where we ourselves were visible from afar. We enjoyed seeing the villages which stood like eagles' nests on the ridge above the river. It was country which could be held, even against superior numbers. We crossed another steep ravine, where Fyodor held up the cart by sitting on his hindlegs. Then I went to report to the Reuber Battalion, which is called after its commander "Reuber Hauptmann". Everybody was still asleep. The enemy had not yet come close. However, there were signs of life four houses away. It was the O.P., and Lieutenant R. was talking on the wireless to his forward observer far away with an outpost.

I looked for a house, set up our own wireless communication, and then shuttled between the gun position, the O.P. and my billet.

In the meantime the outpost had made contact with the enemy. The observer repelled a couple of small attacks with the aid of a gun battery, at the same time misleading the enemy about the position of the new line. He also counted their numbers, the long marching columns which were approaching on various roads and the advance parties pushing carefully and gingerly into the villages.

The outpost withdrew. Act two opened with our bombardment. The first village began burning, others followed But we didn't play that game *ad nauseam*. It was enough that the enemy was delayed for a time by having to deploy his troops. My orders to change position arrived in the early afternoon. We packed up and left.

We could still trek happily across an open hillside. However, we now walked singly and with a little distance between us. Soon another road was leading us back; the ford across the Dnieper was no longer usable. The sky was clear blue, the sun strong. A mighty thaw had set in. The snow became soggy and the snow water ran across the roads. We had to cross some vile ravines. Twice the horse and cart went into a downhill slide. Fyodor was breathing like a locomotive. We had to give him several rests. At the regiment they were keeping open the last communications by wireless. When after many detours we finally reached the *Rollbahn*, it had been dark for some hours and our unit had passed through long before.

I went ahead with a lorry, hoping to catch up with them, but it was too late. At midnight I decided to stay in Ch., because a night-march into the unknown is a doubtful proposition in this country. Also we were very tired. Despite the wind and cold, Jean was almost falling off the driver's seat. His face was like a mask, distorted by the effort of staying awake. We reached the nearest prepared position. There we found a stable for the horse, and room for ourselves by the stove with some infantry boys.

I fetched the guitar. The firelit faces made a bright circle with the bodies of the men grouped round in a close ring.

Next day we marched on. We got to the great *Rollbahn*. Our feet weren't used to the cobbles and they hurt. But the carts rolled easily. Despite the cold and the speed of the march, fatigue overtook us again like an anaesthetic. Sometimes we saw searchlights ahead, or parachute flares, or the explosions of bombs. In between there was only the wind on the dark plain, the clack of the hooves and the rumble of the wheels.

As the sky in the East was turning green, we swung off the road and marched into the village which was to be our new area. The morning before we had marched twenty kilometres trying to catch up with the section, now we had done seventy. Between friends, that was quite enough. We didn't mind the village consisting of miserable, bug-infested shacks. We didn't mind its being overcrowded, so long as there was room to squeeze in somewhere. I took my pack and my blankets and went slowly into the red sun, towards the house where our headquarters were.

On March the 14th we took a walk along our new line, the line which must be held. They have prepared it well. The dugouts are almost finished and the ground has been surveyed. It's a miserable tract of country, undistinguished by anything remarkable. But beyond the line the villages are being burnt down, and the bed we have made for the enemy won't be very comfortable. Our own position is good by comparison.

Day after day we've been out in the brilliant sunshine, walking over the frozen fields where the first larks are rising. We don't count on contact with the enemy before the eighteenth.

At night I put on my woollen helmet, a scarf for a face-covering and gloves for my hands. The bugs fall off the ceiling down your neck. They come on to the table, brown and hungry and next minute they're marching up your wrists. Lieutenant O. spears them with a needle and holds them over the candle, curling his upper lip in disgust. The ceiling has been plastered with a collection of last year's illustrated papers, together with an odd collection of Russian newspapers and torn strips of wallpaper. There's the Fuehrer's car driving at us, Stalin threatening us with his square head, women smiling and soldiers attacking on the battlefields of the earth. It's like a dim mirror in which the mask of these apocalyptic years has been caught in a terrible rigor mortis.

Away to the East the enemy is attacking more strongly. Sometimes the sounds of battle blow over here, and the familiar double thud of a tank hit seems to be eating its way along the front. We sniff the wind and take in the scent. But the enemy is feeling his way towards our sector very slowly.

Today he made contact with our forward strong points, which are holding up his advance beyond the outposts proper. They're there to camouflage the new line. He is not quite within range of our howitzers yet, but our guns can reach him, and at night an air

O.P. goes up and directs them onto the Russian camp fires which shine up out of the solitude.

The enemy can't do without these fires. It's hard weather in which to be without a roof, marching all the time into the unknown, never with dry feet or dry clothing, with bread that never comes up and guns that don't come forward, because the bridges have been blown and the roads have been ruined by the German columns. So you have to get round a fire at night, and you're too tired to realise that there's somebody in the sky like a malicious insect, directing the shells till fire falls on fire.

The stars are drowned in the disembodied light which fills the milky blue sky. Once again there's an incomparable spectacle of colours from fires of the last remaining villages before the main firing line. The air is so still that one can almost feel the terrible heat. Then, after a few hours, the fires subside and mingle with the blue of the night to form deep reds and violets.

On March the 22nd, 1943, I was promoted Lieutenant with effect from March the 1st. They haven't yet decided on my seniority, but for the moment I've been given command of an artillery survey section with my old regiment.

In the past few days the enemy has been slowly filtering into the areas we have prepared for him. On the evening of the twenty-first the companies in the advanced strong points were pulled back to the ordinary outpost line, and now we have begun shelling. To-night, for the first time, a small group of enemy got round our outpost and ran into our wire. They left eighteen dead and two prisoners. Gradually the front is livening up. Machine-guns, mortars, and the enemy's anti-tank guns. Our own guns overshadow everything. Their voice is mightier than anything else, and the trajectories focus on the target area like the rays of the sun falling through a lens.

Today a senior Russian artillery staff fell into the hands of one of our outposts. They drove blindly into the position with a lorry. Unfortunately they had already passed through the machine-guns, so they were shot to pieces. However, a captain, *aide-de-camp* to a senior artillery officer, has deserted to us; he gave us important details about the enemy, as well as encouraging particulars about the success of our defence.

End of March. There's a wet wind with low-hanging clouds, and the trenches are full of water. The snow gets shabbier every day. As soon as the topsoil thaws, it dissolves into a muddy soup and hangs about on the hard ground beneath. Ammunition supply is getting difficult. It's hard on the horses. Our daily expenditure is ten times that of the enemy, who so far has only been able to bring up some light infantry pieces. Today we withdrew our outpost.

I am sitting here writing all this down for the unit war diary. Events, dates, figures. It's an unexciting job. There are the files and notes of months on the table, and the little typewriter stands in the middle waiting to be fed. I don't feel like it at all today. A small bug runs across the table in full daylight and ends up as a red spot. But there are plenty more—tiny, transparent ones, as small as autumn spiders, and dark, revolting ones, which we spear, and whose bellies swell in the candle flame before they explode. Often we jump off our chairs and tear off our jackets because yet another little bastard is sitting in the collar band.

My depression lasted until I was cheered up by a conversation which one of the men was having next door with Wilhelm, our young auxiliary. Wilhelm is fifteen, and he joined us in Rzhev. He ran away from his mother, and now the German soldiers are bringing him up in their own rough, fatherly way. They talk to him in a language of their own, and it's funny to hear. "What you do?" they say. "When you wash last time? Yesterday? You go wash! You go fetch water, you Russian!" And Wilhelm laughs and goes off. He has grown full and round in the face, he laughs with his narrow eyes, and at night he sleeps at the soldiers' feet, the sleep of his fifteen years.

Sometimes it's said that war makes people undisciplined and

violent, that soldiers may find it difficult to go back one day to an ordered life. That is nonsense. It's true that the war has destroyed the old scheme of things in our inner selves, and has demanded a new assessment of values. It blighted our sensibility like a frost. But equally you can say that it makes people simple and good, that it purifies the soul, because the war has shown us the values which count when everything else breaks down: humanity, the brotherhood of suffering, comradeship between men.

Since three this morning our telephone hasn't had a chance to cool off. The enemy is attacking along the whole line. He doesn't seem to realise that he's now come up against a line that's going to be held. Otherwise there's no way of explaining this feeble effort. It's true that there's some lively artillery activity, and his Stalin organ has arrived here too. But he can't possibly afford this expenditure of ammunition for very long. You can't organise a supply system from one day to the next through a devastated country of blown bridges, wrecked railway lines and roads sunk in mud. So let him come. We aren't worried.

During the night some small enemy forces got into our position and were thrown out thirty minutes later by a counter-attack. All other attacks were repelled and since midday Ivan has calmed down a bit.

Our observers can see over the enemy's supply roads and form-ing-up areas; the air O.P., which has been up since morning, does the rest. As far as ammunition goes, we have the longer wind; Ivan never gets a proper word in. His divisions are the same ones which met us at Rzhev, plus a few more. All told, there are five of them, plus two artillery regiments. The latter have brought up a respectable number of guns in the last few days, but the divisions are badly battered. In any case, Ivan ought to know that he hasn't enough for an assault, even if he counts in the miserable remnants of a tank brigade, which are hardly worth talking about. Before we take him seriously, he'll have to bring up quite a bit more and not economise on armour.

As I was all by myself at this early hour, I thought I might use the typewriter to have a chat with you. One doesn't have to think hard, and it fits in so well with this morning which has at last brought a fresh wind and pale sunlight again. The yellow stubble makes a bright splash of colour, and across the fields of this one-time collective farm there is the first shimmer of young corn. The last lumps of snow in the shadowed corners can't get the better of it any more. These are the days in the year when we suddenly feel that the force of nature is at work again, that our field, too, will again be ploughed into new fruitfulness. It's the dispensation of grace after these god-forsaken months. And so I am light of heart today.

Over on the crest of the brown hill, there are two men walking with heavy poles. They carry them on their bent backs, and the poles point over their heads into the light sky, like the poles of the local draw-wells. All this strikes me as worth noticing and telling you about. I don't know if you want to hear about it—the black, rich furrow which a tractor has torn in this meagre stubble field, the little space of warmth at the bottom of the river gully, the lark above the field or a hazel-bush in blossom—I only know that they have something to say to me in this countryside which is so sparing with its charms. "How could you stand it so long up here?" I was asked by someone who came from the Southern front a little while ago. But it's very simple: if you don't have abundance, you must be happy with little things, and a single bloom can mean more than a whole flower-bed.

We spent four weeks building our headquarters. Today we moved in. It's not the only respectable building in the area, but it's pretty good. It lies on the south slope of a small depression. The three rooms are connected by a corridor on the valley side. The windows open towards the South, and between them are two approach trenches cut cleanly into the slope, so that from the outside it already has a certain architectural harmony about it. The land slopes backwards a little to the small river. A path has been made across the slope to connect headquarters with the dug-outs on either side.

Some nice carpentry went into finishing the dugouts. A wood-carver from the Rhön Mountains made the tables, doors, clothes pegs and comfortably moulded corner-seat. The walls are covered with sacking battened down with slats of birch, strong grey paper has been glued on the ceiling, and there are recesses in the walls for books. The whole thing has a clean and unpretentious style of its own. The command post contains a plotting table, wall-maps and telephones. The other two dugouts are sleeping and living quarters, and are clean, light and spacious. Our dugout construction gets better and better. Now we find it quite natural to arrive somewhere and settle down in the woods or fields. In the old days we'd have thought one needed a house.

We have asked for flower seeds and we're also going to lay out a vegetable garden. We have already planted young firs and shrubs. Soldiers don't generally reap the fruits of their sowing; war and husbandry are two different things. But it's worth start-ing, anyway. It's so tempting.

The air is light and sweet, it's all sunshine, like the calls of the birds. The wind is like a young brother. These are the wonder-ful days between frost and heat, harsh nights and oppressive evenings when we are serenaded by swarms of mosquitoes. These are the year's days of promise. The mud is already drying out, hardening and cracking like plaster. Soon it will crumble to powder beneath feet and wheels and hooves. The first sheets of dust are already blowing across the *Rollbahn*.

24th of April, 1943. Yesterday for the first time the temperature was nearly sixty-eight degrees. Lieutenant von Rühle rode over to the estate which once belonged to his great-uncle. He picked some wild flowers in the park, delicate blue anemones with transparent leaves and white pistils. The sun is shining through our windows, flooding down on the plotting table. P. makes a final adjustment to our range map, which covers eighteen kilometres. He dusts the map with foot powder so that the water colour we use to cover up wrong entries doesn't run. He's got his own method, one of our many makeshift techniques.

The front is quiet. What firing there is, is ours.

We have quite a lot of work. Our air-link wireless was receiving yesterday from 0100 to 0300, and from 0500 to 1800. It often does the fire control for three batteries on three different targets simultaneously. According to our own observers and the statements of deserters, the result is excellent.

In honour of Easter we have decorated our sleeping quarters with strips of birch. We have put up some pictures and fixed a couple of vases to the walls. One is a little metal mug kept in place by three pencils, the other an old tin which I wrapped in paper. We put hazel twigs in them, and their leaves are turning towards the light. We can lie comfortably on our palliasses on our home-made beds. We even have a white linen sheet each, plus a blue-checked overlay and pillowcase. At night I can take off my trousers and go to bed dressed only in my shirt. Perhaps it's not easy for you to understand what that means, but I can tell you, every night I'm grateful for it.

So this is Easter Sunday. It can be like that. The men are lying in the grass of the hollow, or squatting on their heels, blinking into the light and laughing at the coarse jokes of a concert party. The sun collects here as if caught in the hollow of one's hand. The taut air vibrates in the sunlight. Behind the hollow a cornfield rises. You can see the tender green shoots growing from day to day. They breathe in the moist, warm air and the green grows darker. In the birch woods the first gleam of the young leaves mingle with the wintry grey. It's as if a breath of life were passing over it. On many fields last year's grass is still lying yellow and dry like an old man's hair, but underneath the shoots are swelling mightily. Today the spring's first thunderstorms passed over the land in a changing light. They seem shorter and more violent than at home, but perhaps it's only because one can see the whole extent of them. They fill the whole sky with their amazing force, dominating the whole countryside, so that when they're gone its breadth emerges in all its splendour. Once great hailstones sprang across the road, but afterwards the moist earth steamed with fertility, gleaming like a horse after a good run. Soon we'll plough and sow the summer corn, even here, in the front line.

Our life has its periods. When the years run out, irrevocably, completely, one can only clench one's teeth. It's childish to think that we can be recompensed for them. Because all the possibilities that are lost during the passing of this period will never be retrieved. No one can sow in summer. But perhaps, too, it's childish to discuss this question. I tell myself this because in this war, more than in any war before, one's thoughts revolve round the meaning of what is happening. My own attitude is far from certain. But here, in one of the greatest chapters of the history of mankind, must surely be the final demonstration of the Prussian spirit—in that the finest part of the German people are facing the inevitable with open eyes, that they accept as inescapable a call which in one important respect exceeds what was demanded of the soldiers of 1914. We are living through a soul-chilling experience.

We drove to our forward echelon. The sun was smiling and the driving wind clapped happily around us. The motor-cycle combination swayed over the cart tracks and turned towards the *Rollbahn*. Franz Wolff dismounted, and with the engine humming quietly we slithered over the roots below the last tall fir trees. Then we switched off. The wind had dropped. The sun fell diagonally through the trees and showered the camp with a wave of light. There was a smell of resin and horses. The area between the stables had been swept clean. The block houses and round tents were lying peacefully, distributed round the perimeter. In the middle was the clearing where the auxiliaries[1] had gathered to be

---

[1] Volunteers recruited among Russian prisoners and incorporated in existing German units to meet the manpower shortage.

sworn in. They looked smart in their tunics with white arm-bands and their caps without a badge. Clean and well nourished.

The interpreter was a young Russian. He came noiselessly through the wood, his rifle slung loosely over his shoulder, a lean, tanned face above an open collar, and with those animal-like movements which combine endurance with agility. He spoke well, raising his head from the script and underlining words with sparse gestures. The auxiliaries stood dressed in an open square and listened with tense concentration. "Is it right, what I have read out to you?" he said. "*Pravda*," they nodded, "it's the truth." Their faces hardened. They took their oath without hesitation, binding themselves to go on serving us faithfully, just as they had served us since they joined us or were taken prisoner, way back in Smolensk or Kalinin or Rzhev. They know that they haven't made a bad bargain. You have only to look at them.

But they said they had a few questions and I told them: "Go ahead."

Were they now on an equal footing with the German soldiers? some of them asked. They were thinking of the schnapps ration: it wasn't difficult to read that from their faces. So I asked them through the interpreter whether they had ever gone hungry in all their time with us. They laughed, all of them—and we were friends. Others asked if they could get transferred to Vlasov's Army[1] and they persisted with their question. They weren't many, but they were the best; they were men worth looking at, their enquiries were clear and precise, and with their calloused hands they signed their names with a fluency and confidence you would never have expected.

The sunlight flooded through the fir trees, the chaffinches wagged their tails and the tits were making a noise in the branches, as we sat by the little hut in the wood and talked for a long time about many things connected with all this.

[1] The army of Russian volunteers to be set up under the former Soviet General Vlasov. The project was opposed by Hitler. (For its further history see *The Soviet Army*, edited by B. H. Liddell Hart.)

CHAPTER XIII

AN ISLAND IN THE PALM OF GOD'S HAND

Between April and July there was a lull. The Russians, whose attack had come to a halt, were waiting for the Germans to make the first move in a summer offensive. The Germans, however, took three months to assemble the necessary reserves.

WITH von Rühle I rode through the cool May morning. As we went down into a dip, the woods and villages which had been our landmarks disappeared, to reappear over the crest of the hills as the horses climbed the slope beyond. Then there was that feeling of breadth again. We are always in the centre of this wide landscape. The saddle creaks, you feel the warmth of horseflesh between your legs, your eye is free to rove.

An hour's ride ahead of us we could see the church with the round top of its tower rising above the estate. So that was Sasishyo, once the country-seat of a Russian prince, later the manor house of my companion's great-uncle. Some stables were still standing. The plaster was crumbling from the walls, but they were large and spacious and built in stone, witnesses to a former prosperity. Nothing had been done since then. An ugly concrete shed was all that the Sovchose administration had added for the improvement of the estate. Then the war clamped down on it.

But what an estate it once had been. The ruins of about two dozen large buildings, not counting the wooden houses, were scattered over an area of one hundred and twenty acres. Between the stables and the farm-buildings the drive went up towards the house which stood at the south end of the property in the park. It was a single-storied building. Even today the remains of the mellow walls form a semi-circle round a lawn with a drive of young limes. In front of it was the guest house. To the east a narrow street ran between small houses towards the church which belonged to the estate. It stood at one end of the grounds, so that the view was not allowed to extend into the far distance and man could find the peace of finity and shelter.

On his first visit, von R. had already found an old man who remembered his great-uncle: "Ah, the old times, sir!" Barefooted children greeted us, girls laughed, men looked up from their work: "*Sdravstvuytye*," said the old ones. The young ones smiled at us and said: "Goot morrning."

We rode, enchanted, through the park, down the narrow central avenue which leads from the house towards the Dnieper plain. Old trees arched over it to form a dark tunnel which only opened out far down in the sun-drenched fields. Left and right, shrubberies and lawns shimmered through the trees, bordered by weather-beaten oaks, firs, limes and spruce. The air drifted in gentle waves, insects were buzzing and birds flew off with vivid little cries. Sweet peas, crowsfoot, nettles and anemones flowered along the winding paths. The air stood still. Mosquitoes sang over the wilderness. Yet among all the exuberant weeds you could still feel the orderly hand which once was master.

Once more we stood on the high hill, the horses' heads resting on our shoulders as we watched the clouds sail over the sunlit countryside. Would that God would give us back the earth so that we could work again.

How full these days have been. Yesterday, with short interruptions, I was on horseback from half-past one till half-past nine at night. First I was at the echelon to look at the horses and see how the work was going on. Then in Area Two to see if the salad was ready for cutting and how the radishes were to be distributed. I also had to arrange for the salad to be delivered to-day, and to see whether the civilians were getting their compensation in food as I had ordered. Finally I had to have a talk with my man there about a very difficult problem in his private life. I came back here to evaluate the result of my visit and spent half an hour taking a cup of coffee with the Vet. Then I rode with one of our high-ups, a theologist, to the field cinema. It was walk and trot, walk and trot. Ten minutes before the show was due to start I slid from the steaming horse and shook hands with Heini Steubing, who had kept seats for us. The hut was crammed to bursting point. Two minutes later the General sat down beside me. I was greeted by the grins of my men, the scoundrels. I had given them passes; they had marched seven kilometres and, following my advice, had smuggled themselves in without tickets.

Back with a rumbling stomach: walk, trot, gallop: don't fall, little horse! Dusk fell, the potholes were treacherous, wretched telephone wires. We went all the time across country. Ratsch bummm!—an anti-tank gun. Machine-gun bullets—the music of the front line—guns in the night—silent hunched animals—sentry standing tall against the light sky. On we trotted—a cart track—a bridge—Wren pricked up his ears, we were at the stable. My batman came running, he knew my horse's step in the night.

It was the winter of 1941. Captain H. was riding ahead of the battery. It was very cold. He went into a house to warm himself. "*Cholodna*," he said, rubbing his hands. "You may speak German," answered a woman who came towards him out of the dark room. They started to talk. She said she had worked for five years on an estate in Holstein.—"But how can you bear to live here with one bed, three pots, a couple of forks and a knife, now that you know what life is like in Germany?"—"We live, too," the woman answered. . . .

The other day we were in the billet. "Olga, do you want to see some pictures? Come here, I show you some!" said my

163

companion. Olga came at once. She wanted to know a lot about that curious Germany, of which she had heard so much. "That's my daughter—look—she's seven months old now," my companion explained. "Good," said Olga, her woman's liking for children melting her reserve for a moment. "But that's not the same child," she said suddenly, reaching for the next snapshot. "This child is much bigger than the first."

"But, Olga," said my companion, "the second picture has been taken from a closer distance. Don't you see that?"

She looked at him dubiously, shaking her head a little and scrutinising the picture again. "Is that your wife? Good," she said critically. "But *that* isn't her," she said, reaching for the next one. "Why not?"—"No," laughed Olga, "you try to trick me. In this picture she has a quite different handbag. You see, you slipped up."

She listened suspiciously to his explanations, she couldn't believe it. We looked thoughtfully at the girl. Then we looked round the room, this Russian peasant's room, which was once dark and musty and had now been turned by the German soldiers into a clean billet. And we knew that we had a long way to go yet.

We were at the echelon, doing a kit inspection. The Battery Commander was inspecting the auxiliaries. "Where's your tunic, Alexey?" "At the tailor's, sir." "Off you go and fetch it." Alexey turned about smartly and disappeared like lightning. He was back in a second. He clicked his heels and suppressed his breathlessness. It didn't do for it to be seen that he had been running hard. Alexey is a passionate soldier. He had sewn a badge on his cap; it would wound his honour deeply if we were to take it away. He wears his uniform in a way of his own, but he wears it with the pride of a child. He keeps up his trousers with a belt and pushes down the tops of his boots so that the leather lies in folds round the ankles. He wears his spurs high in the Cossack manner. It's difficult to talk him out of it. Even the ill-fitting tunic and trousers can't hide his lithe body. He isn't just anybody. When he came back from the swearing-in he said: "I won't be with the battery long, I'm going to Vlasov. Just wait and see."

Two villages further on we met Grigoryi. He was fourteen years old. They had picked him up on his wanderings, leading two women and two children. He came into the Battery Commander's office as if we were old friends. "Where are you going?" —"Home to Nikitnia, sir." He took off his cap. A shock of blond hair appeared. From his lean boyish face two clear eyes were laughing. "The Dokyumenti?"—"Here." He laid down the papers and stepped back, waiting, watchful and tense while we deciphered them. There it was, right enough: "Grigoryi B. and mother Lyuba B., daughter Maria; Walya S. with child, proceeding from Smolensk hospital to Nikitnia."

Grigoryi stood in front, the others behind him. "Quiet, Mother!" he said, when the woman behind his back started to move. He didn't turn round, but merely made an impatient gesture with his hand. The mother's eyes rested full of pride on her son. "In order?" he asked, and it sounded as if he weren't leaving us any choice. "In order, Grigoryi," we nodded. . . . "Cigarette?"

Then his tension relaxed for a moment, his eyes lit up and he bent over the officer's shoulders to take a light from the Battery Commander. He stepped back and pulled at his cigarette like a man dying of thirst. Then he started to talk. His answers came quickly and frankly to the personal questions we were putting. Finally he said, "Well!" and touched his cap, full of confidence between man and man as he left the room to have quarters assigned to him. It sounded funny and boyish, this expression which he had picked up. But Grigoryi the man had already sent the women ahead. When he had seen to his charges he came back: did we have some potatoes for them?—Yes, he could have some. —How about some bread?—That wasn't so easy, we told him. He didn't lament, as they do sometimes in this country; he didn't tell us the long story of their suffering. He just looked at us and said: "Two hundred grammes!"

Two hundred grammes; that meant: Master, you know we have nothing to eat, don't you? I know it's war, but I don't ask much for five people. We're used to a hard life. It's not our fault that we have nothing to eat.

Need I say that he got his bread—and that the Battery Commander cut it off his own rations?

I couldn't help remembering how often during the first summer we enjoyed the spontaneous hospitality of Russian peasants, how without our asking they would set their modest food before us because we had come to them tired and thirsty and burnt out by the sun. I remembered countless occasions on which a little friendliness was repaid by silent devotion. I saw once more a woman's tears on her worn face, releasing a whole load of misery, when I gave her child a sweet. I felt on my hair the timid hand of an old grandmother, as she received me, the dreaded first soldier, with many bows and an old-fashioned kiss on the hand. How her heart overflowed because I liked her food and merely told her how much I enjoyed it. Or again, I remembered the man who was so proud to receive us, the day we lagged far behind the battery with our worn-out horses and fled from a thunderstorm into his village off the main road. He looked after the horses and distributed us over the best families in the village for lunch—all because he had once spent four years as a prisoner-of-war in Germany. He told us of his youth. "In Siberia," he said, "the peasants left their houses open even when they were out in the fields, and on the table there was always bread and salt for anybody who passed by. At night there would be food on the window-sill for the fugitives from exile walking back to their homes." He drank and sang melancholy songs; all these people are homesick.

One has to see them in an hour like this to know of what veneration and devotion they are capable, and to feel from what simple hearts their actions spring.

They serve you so naturally and devotedly that you are

continually surprised. The old mother comes of her own accord to wash up the mess-tins. The grandfather with his curly head and wild beard needs only a word to send him off for water; he carried it in quantities which he finds unbelievable. He does everything we need and smiles apologetically when he has to stop to warm his frozen hands, letting thick icicles drip on to the stove from his beard. "Forgive me, Master, I'm old," he smiles sadly. They shovel snow, cut wood, peel potatoes, stick branches beside the paths. Everything works smoothly and by itself. At the battery we have several prisoners who look after the horses and help at the field kitchen. They wear white arm-bands and carry an identity card. It never seems to occur to them that things might be different. The old man sits behind me in a corner, gratefully smoking a cigarette which he has rolled from our fag-ends and a piece of newspaper. They sit beside us spooning their soup while we, by their standards, live in abundance. And they find nothing wrong with it. No dark looks, not the slightest antagonism. "*Spacibo, Pan,*"—thank you, Master. They say it for the least thing. Happy children's eyes and a low bow for smallest present: Germanski soldier good.

We burn down their houses, we take their last cow from the shed and the last potatoes from their cellars. We pull off their felt shoes, and often they're shouted at and roughly treated. Yet always they have packed their bundles and gone away with us, from Kalinin and from all the villages along the road. We had to detail special people to take them to the rear. Anything rather than be on the other side! What a schism, what a contrast. What must these people have suffered. What a mission it could be to give them back order and peace, work and bread!

The days pass quickly without great tension. But much is happening within us, and I only wish I had time enough to put it all down. However, I'm very well—my health couldn't be better.

Our garden is doing well. The lettuces are still a little blue because the nights are too cold. But everything is coming up, if a little slowly, and in the meantime we have an excellent kind of spinach made from nettles. I should write a paper on garden- ing. But then there are so many things still waiting to be written up, and time is divided into so many little pieces.

It's evening, the end of another day of little joys and worries, that's to say, if you call it a *little* joy to put all you have into leading your men. It's a task that calls for constant readiness, kindness, a firm grip and an instinct for essentials. What a mix- ture of wisdom and firmness it needs to lead men in the third year of the war! But what a vocation too! It fills me with happiness to feel that I have the power to release so many forces for good, that men comes to me with confidence. Their faces brighten when they see me and they become cheerful and at ease with themselves when I pass by them with a word of greeting. One must have the right word at the right moment. How right you are, Mother. As I write this down I remember that it's something you have just said yourself.

It's Sunday. For the past three days I have been in temporary command of Headquarters Battery. Early in the morning I rode down a telephone line to the Twelfth to take a bath. I had quite a time of it at a trench, where Wren reared up three times on his hind-legs before going over trembling and blowing. The first time we fought with each other for a quarter of an hour before he gave in. We were both pretty wet afterwards. We had hardly left the gun position when it was plastered by enemy Heavies. Fragments and lumps of earth splashed into the water left and right of the ford where we had taken cover. When I gave him rein in a lull in the firing, he raced up the slope and took the trench without hesitation.

Afterwards I went through the dugouts and met Corporal Karl, who reported back two days ago from a job which had taken him away from the battery for almost a year. Karl is a tall blond chap, an example of a good comrade and a good soldier. "Well, how do you like being back with the old gang?" I asked him. "Sir," he said, searching for the right words—"when I came back I noticed it right away, and the boys say the same: there's a new atmosphere here altogether."

Isn't it worth it to live a life like this? My days are so full that they seem to run into each other. My leave lies far behind me, and although the longing sometimes overtakes me I soon get over it. Every day we feel anew that this summer is a gift to us. We live for the present.

I was lying on the slope by the dugout. It was midday. The blanket beneath me was burning hot. There was hardly a breath of wind. Insects darted glistening through the air. They made a sound like the soft hum of an organ. My thoughts were engulfed in waves of light purple, and dreams unfolded their red sails. I don't know how long I had been lying there, when the handset of the telephone slipped off and knocked my shoulder. I jerked up swaying in a trance. What was it? Wasn't that Pan's black-and-white goat-face above me with its malicious mouth? He stared at me, motionless and sneering, with his yellow eyes, surrounded by nodding grasses, and the wind played in his scanty beard.

Goat-god Pan, do you venture this far East? But then the tele-phone started talking, and I realised it was only our little goat. He hopped and skipped away after his foster-father till his thin bleats were lost in the noon-day. I followed him with my eyes, smiling, and picked up the receiver. ". . . Hello, Pan-pipe."— "Is that Lute?"—"Prepare for action!"—And the goat-god's play was silenced by the song of our big guns.

I walked through the heat towards our garden. It is set in the midst of the wild fields like an island in the palm of God's hand. I felt the touch of the earth on my bare feet. It is strange to be able to lay out gardens here in the front line, and we are grateful. The men's faces as they bend over the plants are relaxed and peaceful. We have always missed salad and vegetables in our rations, and it was an act of cool calculation to plant one hundred and twenty acres of oats and potatoes in the echelon area.

But the joy of the work was obvious and many of us had additional seeds sent from home. In the evenings our dug-out community stand round their little flower bed, and beneath their uncouth irony they open the secret doors of their hearts. Why else should they have sown flowers? It's sheer pleasure to see how they follow the progress of sun-flowers, mignonette, nasturtiums, asters and humble calendula. I know it has been said before, but the serenity of plants means more than ever to one in these times when the sacred order of things has been disrupted.

In normal times I would now come in with a bunch of fresh flowers. It's a pity that I can't do it. Not only could I walk over these fields picking the most wonderful bouquet, but I could even bring flowers of my own growing, delicate poppies which open their petals in the morning, red and yellow and violet. If only I could bring them to you. You know how I have always picked from their abundance at home and given them to everyone who shared my joy.

In the evenings, when the plants are thirsty, we go down to the little stream with jugs and buckets, and we do our watering with cans pierced through the bottom. The hollow is filled with the laughter of men pouring water over each other's heads. In the still air among the bushes the gnats perform their dance of the thin veils. But they don't worry us much, because there's always a wind, and there's no discordant note in this great symphony of water and sunlight, of scented grass and warm nights, and of this peace which hangs over the sector like the great dome of a bell.

I was in the camp in the wood when I got my mail, and had no time to read it. When at last I managed to do so, we had ridden a long way and Wren and I were hurrying homewards. The reins lay on his neck, and from time to time I would brush

170

away the mosquitoes. The track made a black ribbon through the moist grass, which stretched away on both sides, green and yellow and violet, with bright patches of bluebells and crowsfoot. But when I put down the piece of paper, there were only the red panicles of sorrel against the setting sun, like countless small hearts.

Then I gave Wren a dig with the spurs.

CHAPTER XIV

ON THE HIGHROAD

THE enemy's front line has remained practically unchanged lately. It's the same with his artillery, which is about equal to ours. Tanks have rarely appeared. It's the quietest sector we have ever had. All the same, the enemy has been lively with patrols. In June we drove back thirty-six of them plus an attack in battalion strength south of Pyshtshenka on the 24th, when he lost two hundred and forty out of three hundred and sixty men.

On July the 1st an enemy patrol of between thirty and forty men penetrated the infantry lines by the advanced O.P. of No. 12 Battery. The attack was a surprise and came after only a short artillery preparation with mortars and light guns. It was at 0430. The infantry made a temporary withdrawal from the point of penetration. The advanced observer's line was out of order and he had to run to company headquarters to call for fire over the infantry line. The enemy patrol surprised his signallers in the dugout where they were trying to establish communication. The telephone was shot to pieces and the enemy took it away with them. The wireless operator managed to hide himself, but the patrol got the set and the observer's artillery map. They also took away one of our dead infantrymen. They left their own dead behind. We put down eighty-seven rounds in defence. In the trench and in front of the wire they counted twenty-four enemy dead in the evening.

It must have been wishful thinking when we imagined we should be left alone this summer. Of course we were wrong. We are going back into the melting-pot once more. Not that we shrink from it! We still possess the secret energy which quickens our movements and steadies our voices when we smell danger.

Before us lie the summer and a third winter. Some people still refuse to see it that way. They refuse to accept the idea that they will have to go on without leave. I myself stand aside with a little smile and watch events taking their course. Everything goes according to plan—the plan mapped out by fate. We are only cogs. The century is going through its sickness. It remains to be seen if it has the strength to overcome the chaos. I maintain my calm—a calm which doesn't try to fight against things but goes through them as if through a transformation in which nothing is changed in our character except that we achieve a deeper understanding of ourselves. I have no anxiety about myself, the life imposed on us is easy and there are always our day-to-day duties. It only makes me sad that *you* will be hurt, I'm a little afraid you may get tired and lose the lustre of tranquillity. I am not tired. The black hours are few and far between. The Division isn't tired either. Some people think it is, but it's only hope which drives them—the hope and dream of home. They'll be disappointed. The Division is no more worn out than any other. There'll be no relief for us, I'm sure of that. But the summer will be easier, and once more it will be a case of seeing flowers and grasses instead of heat and dust. As Jo puts it so well: "Some see the hoar-frost, the pale moon and perhaps a cat as it stalks through the darkness; others see only the frost on the bushes. There's no special merit in it, it's a way of living. We just happen to be made that way." It gives you a great strength. I'm glad of it, Jo.

The German attack was launched, on the Southern Sector, on 5th of July with seventeen armoured divisions—all that could be mustered. The Russians, however, were waiting behind extensive minefields, with their main forces withdrawn behind the front line. Within seven days the Germans started to pull out. Almost at once the Russians opened their counter-offensive, and by the end of the month it extended to the Central Sector. At this point Pabst's division, which seems to have been in reserve in the Smolensk area, was hurriedly called South-East to help stop the Russians cutting German communications behind Orel. The effort succeeded by a narrow margin, but Orel had to be abandoned on August 5th. The retreat which followed was slow at first but gathered disorder as the Germans were harassed by aircraft above and by partisans and infiltrating groups on the ground. It swept Pabst back through Bryansk, across the Desna, and North-West to the great Moscow–Minsk highway, there to meet in an obscure and unrecorded action the death which had so often occupied his thoughts.

At 0730 we left Gridino and moved up to the *Rollbahn*. The sky was overcast, visibility bad, and rain crept up on us noiselessly. We glanced for the last time at our gardens and the friendly hills before our vehicles changed their course. The horses went steadily ahead, round and glossy from their long period of rest. We marched fast. At 1300 we reached Yartsevo and halted amid the remains of big buildings. We stood on the grass verges of a miserable avenue facing the stump of a plaster monument, a relic of proletarian culture. The field kitchen was steaming. At 1500 we began to entrain. The ramp was wide enough to take nearly all the vehicles of the fighting echelon. Everything went quickly. Soon all the vehicles were anchored with wooden blocks and shackling wires. The horses were in their trucks, knee-deep in hay. Between the vehicles bivouacs were going up, because there was not enough room for everybody in the straw by the horses.

Severinov, the Russian auxiliary,[1] came to say goodbye. The changing fortunes of war had made him homeless. He had served for some weeks with the unit and now he wanted to stay with his family who had found work in Yartsevo. He had come to us with a heavy heart, taciturn and reserved, and it struck me that he must be carrying a great burden of sad memories. He had found a kind of foothold with us. Now as he was standing before me,

---

[1] Probably an orderly—not one of those sworn in as a combatant.

174

his long bony hand groped for mine once more. In his grip there was everything he couldn't express with words.

Yet he had to say something, even at the risk of my only half understanding it. He made a kind of little speech, his hand jerking slightly, refusing to let go of mine, and all the time he looked straight into my eyes. His adam's apple rose and fell in his thin throat and, although I hardly understood a word, I understood the meaning. It was good that it should be so.

At 2100 we started moving. Half an hour later I lay down, and I woke for the first time just before midnight.

When we stopped at R. from 0400 to 0600 I had slept enough. I washed under a gushing hydrant. Over the iron bridge which crossed the track, girls were walking with flowers in their hands. Further along the line there were guard posts behind thick palisades, Red Indian style. A strip of woodland on both sides of the track had been cut down to provide a field of observation. Burnt out, rusty skeletons of goods wagons had been rolled over the embankment. Under cover of anti-aircraft guns innumerable transports were rolling towards the front with rations and ammunition. Empty trains were going back. Somewhere five threshing machines stood as if forgotten on a siding.

At eight o'clock I saw the first sun-flowers in D. They were in a garden. The landscape opened wide, we were on our way to B. For a long time the country was devoid of woods, or any other landmarks. It spread into infinity. The hills were gently curved, like the sea on a still day. From time to time there were some birches hung with sad little bunches of leaves like thin shawls on the shoulders of an old woman, and there were small groups of trees in the villages.

The villages were strewn about haphazardly as if they didn't quite know where to end in this endless country. The area was divided into green and yellow strips, and the houses seemed even lower, enclosed by the squares of potatoes and swaying corn. Wind-swept, weather-worn, with sagging thatched roofs, they made a plucked and miserable sight in the dreary light of this day.

The bigger villages, where there were a few factory buildings, looked even more hopeless. But there were occasionally places where streams had cut a bed into the plain—and even very small streams cut astonishingly wide beds. Here one might come suddenly on a steep slope with villages and groups of trees, and these gave the landscape a livelier character.

We went on for a long time through this country, and our faces grew longer. Lack of wood makes war more difficult. But towards the end of the day we brightened up again. There were woods, even if they were mainly swamp-woods. We dangled our legs contentedly from the open doors of the goods wagons. We would not lack wood after all for the dugouts and gun positions: Russia was all right again. At the stations the usual ragged, bare-footed children were begging: *"Pan, give bread!"* In strange contrast, war material of the latest design was rolling by on the tracks beside them. Vast industrial plants rose suddenly in the woods, and even if only the tall chimneys were standing amid burnt-out sheds and mountains of rubble, the tension between the two worlds was only too obvious—the senseless difference between a tower stuck with balconies like swallows' nests, the Soviet ideal of a living machine, and the wretched thatched huts of the peasants.

But what concern was it of ours? We were waging war. In the weeks to come we should have no time to pursue such thoughts as these. The bottle went round. H. was leaning by the window, his profile set against the evening sky. The weather-worn skin was taut on his finely sculptured head. It made him look like a skeleton, like a mask of tense determination.

We spent nearly all day waiting outside B., whose tall buildings rise high above the banks of a river. Till darkness fell we made music in one of the wagons with a violin, a clarinet, an accordion and my guitar. Later we lay down in the straw, only to wake up and fall asleep again with the movement of the train.

At 0400 we reached our destination. It was July the 31st. We looked out on an overgrown station, whose only remarkable feature was the military loading ramp. From the woods a column of carts appeared, one vehicle after another, at a quick trot and always at the same distance from each other. They disappeared round the next turning like an apparition from another world.

We off-loaded the vehicles and marched to the village, where we rested till 0730. Then we marched for a long time. The landscape opened up, richer and more expansive than it had first appeared. The Vet was riding at my side and said it reminded him of the Ukraine.

Far ahead we could hear the dull rumble of the front, strong and threatening as at the best of times. We moved with long vehicle intervals through the heat of the close day. Everything seemed so familiar, the sweat and the sand, the short rests and the anxiety about the horses, the thirst and the meal stops beside the road. Fighter squadrons hummed towards the enemy in the blue sky, and there were dark explosion-clouds in the woods ahead of us. A thunderstorm broke with a roar, but the weather remained oppressive and the glare of the heat hung over the ripe fields in the wide, shimmering countryside. The horses breathed heavily, their chests flecked with foam as they strained to pull the carts. Most of the time I was riding ahead, following the signs which marked our road. They led us along the *Rollbahn* and then over sandy tracks until, late in the afternoon, we reached a forgotten village. It was lying on the edge of the swamp-woods. The signs lapsed into silence and we halted without knowing how long we should stay there. We looked dubiously at the sky, dispersed and camouflaged the vehicles and were just leading the horses away when the Ratas appeared. They came out of the sun and let us have it. Our machine-guns replied. Then they were gone. No harm had come to us. But behind us in the West there was smoke and fire, and a kilometre ahead our Battery Commander was stuck with his car in the swamp. They had shot the battery to pieces.

We spent the night there, but the night was short. At 0230 we were on the march again, going back the way we had come, because immediately ahead there was no way of getting through. We took all day to reach a place which had been seven kilometres away as the crow flies, and ended up in a bridgehead which our troops had re-taken the day before.

The situation was far from clear. Already I had noticed on the way that there were not many of the supply troops which one usually finds behind a main front. Beyond the swamp-woods along which we were moving there was only a thin line consisting mainly of strong-points for which both sides were fighting with varying success. Between them were intervals of several kilometres. Our troops were only just coming up. The enemy had cut the line of communication down the vital highway, but our counter-attack was already under way. We had to seal off the break. We went into position quickly and without much preparation. We could merely put out sentries and keep our eyes skinned.

In the evening I left the wood by a narrow track to look at a little village which was lying in our immediate neighbourhood and was occupied only by civilians. It had been reported to me that it was still full of young men. That seemed rather suspicious because of the great danger from partisans. It was ideal country for them.

The path led over patches of swampy ground. One had to jump quickly across logs of wood. Without warning one emerged from the wilderness and found oneself in front of the village. It was surrounded by yellow wheat, gleaming barley and dark-green potato plots. It was like an island in the middle of the woods.

In the South-East the ground fell away steeply towards a swampy depression which stretched with low bushes to the river bed, which was the front line. There was no one to be seen there. Beyond the stream began the forest which gave us so much trouble because of its vast extent and thick undergrowth. When you looked at the map you could only see small, widely dispersed villages, crowding on the backs of low-stretched hills. We looked at the ground for a long time and agreed that it would be difficult for the enemy to break through there.

When we turned towards the village and its inhabitants, most of whom were living in dugouts, we saw the usual square of stamped-down earth in front of each house. It had been swept clean and round it stood a semi-circle of corn-sheaves. In the centre of one such square an old man was winnowing wheat. He threw up the grains with a broad wooden shovel, the wind blew the light chaff away and the golden grains fell to the ground. "*Mnogo, mnogo chleb*—much, much bread," he said; you could sense the bounteousness of the earth reflected in his words and the gestures of the people round him.

On a stile a young girl sat looking at me. She wore a bright dress and her eyes were clear and intelligent, and she seemed to me more attractive than any girl I had seen for a long time. But I put aside the thought the moment it entered my head, because I can't permit myself such ideas. The young men who were the object of my visit came ambling towards me. They watched me with half-closed eyes.

But on closer observation I realised that they looked more sinister than they really were, and their confidence grew with the first cigarette. I wondered if it would be necessary to lock them up at nights; it would be awkward if they went across to the enemy. But it was too much bother—I couldn't watch over half Russia. In the end I decided to send my auxiliaries as propagandists. The presence of the girls had already made them restless. The people here are more lively in character than those round Smolensk; they are gayer and more open. Already you can feel the influence of the South. A number of the older women still wear a kind of costume. They wear white kerchiefs arranged like a wimple, with a coloured band over the forehead. At the neckline of their blouses is a narrow, embroidered border, and the sleeves are set into the shoulders with a coloured band about three inches wide. They wear white cloth wound round their calves, bound cross-wise with black ribbons. Underneath protrude their bare feet.

Nearly all the men wear beards. Their heads are covered with unkempt hair which is often also bleached. Hunched on their low pony traps, ragged and barefoot, so low that their feet almost touch the ground, they look like gnomes. With grunts and lashes of the whip they drive their tough ponies, those tormented creatures which are steered by a rope round their mouths. Even the children treat them as though trotting were their normal mode of motion.

I saw an old man driving his horse while he lay on his belly on a load of rye; his eyes shone with glee out of the wild mass of his beard. I saw another who wore a sergeant-major's moustache, whose ends he was always twirling upwards. He told me he had been a prisoner at Mainz during the Great War. I was standing in the middle of the village, distributing sweets to the children. I was about to give a second one to a boy, but he said no, he had had one already and stood back, smiling. Two sweets, think of it, that would be too much. It would be impudent and cheating the friendly stranger. *Pravda*—it's the truth.

At five o'clock the assault on the road to K. was to begin. Up to then there had been no rest. The telephone went all the time. The men had laid many kilometres of cable, but they were on their feet all through the night because of the constant tearing of the lines. Line patrol in the woods presented some difficulty; getting within range of an over-eager sentry in a state of special alert involved considerable danger. Communications over the vast distances in the sector were very bad. Half the talk, as usual, was superfluous. Lieutenant von Rühle shouted and raged, and was several times on the point of smashing the telephone. From time to time the Battery Commander roared like a bear with a sore foot. We were very tired after the march and the day's business, but try as we might, we could get no sleep.

At first light the flap of the tent was thrown back, and the cold morning air streamed in. This time I stayed behind with the doctor, while the others went off to the gun position.

The assault was made simultaneously from the North and the South. The intention was to close a gap of less than two kilometres which contained a bridge, then to push the front so far to the East that the line of communication down the road would be secure. From our side, advancing from the North, the assault moved slowly against stiff resistance on the right flank. Our losses were severe. Enemy snipers, some with machine-guns, sat in the trees till our infantry had passed, and then opened fire from behind. The enemy's tactics were vigorous and elastic. It was impossible to position artillery in the swamp-woods, but he made up the deficiency by the liberal use of mortars.

At the bridge he had dug himself in with a cleverly sited and well-camouflaged defence system which contained, among other things, sixteen built-in flame-throwers. Here we lost our Battery Commander. The commander of one of the Light batteries took over. After artillery preparation by his guns, he rallied the infantry. At the same time, another battalion commander re-formed other units which had been disorganised by heavy casualties and the loss of their officers. So the attack got under way again. On his own initiative, the commander of another Light battery worked his way up from the South with signallers and a few infantry. He got across the bridge and took the enemy positions North-East of it in hand-to-hand fighting. At the same time our left wing had got through the swamp-wood from the North and had broken into the enemy positions by surprise. In this way the junction was made. In the course of the operation Ti. on the East of the road was taken. The unit lost two officers and three men. All walking wounded stayed with us.

Our losses and those of the infantry, particularly in old and experienced soldiers, were an indication of the difficulty and peculiarity of the action.

About midday I was called to tactical headquarters. We moved it to another location in R., which was still under harassing fire and small artillery bombardments. We dug in our tents and the whole fighting echelon came forward. Towards evening it grew quiet. The Pay Sergeant came up and took the first mail away. We sat outside the tent drinking a bottle of wine. It was a lovely *naturreiner* Moselle, and in the quiet of the dusk everything was enveloped by a mood of peace.

After the gap had been closed and the danger of a break-through towards Br. had been averted, communications were slowly established within the regiment. There was news of No. 12 Battery ten kilometres to the South. Meissner, one of their oldest members, had got a scratch too. Franz and I said with a grin that the two of us were long overdue, and since it was Franz's birthday two days before, I got out the bottle I had reserved for the occasion.

Soon after midday we got a message advising us not to go on building. The Division is moving further South down the highway. We're not sorry. We look forward to exchanging this place, which is unfriendly enough, for a better one. There is very lively air activity on both sides. During the night the enemy made a big raid on Br. or O. There was a great deal of rumbling, and the air above us was filled with the tuck-tuck of the slow crude-oilers, which the infantry call coffee-mills or sewing-machines.

The telephonists left at 0300. At five o'clock the gun echelon and horses arrived. We were hardly on the road when the first fighter-attack came. It was no joke, and went on like that all day. The fighters swept happily up and down the road in squadron formations and even bigger. There was a terrific racket on every side and our fighters took a heavy toll of them. But for the men on the road that was no consolation. Needless to say, we had camouflaged the wagons and even the horses. They looked like huts of leaves on the move. We got through without losses in the end, but the Second lost two horses and four men wounded. The new position was a wretched stretch of woods. We had just laid the new lines, a great number of them, and one party had spent two hours laying a one-kilometre length through the swamp when fresh orders came.

Now we are situated close to the regiment, a little way off the road. The dust raised by the traffic comes at us in thick waves. The telephonists sit with their tongues hanging out. They look at me from below their heavy lids like Great Danes. This glowing heat puts a great strain on anyone. The situation in the air hasn't improved. It's a main front line, there's no getting away from the fact. And here we're not even placed at one of the critical points. To the East of us, where the front curves towards O., you can hear it rumbling more seriously. The less said about the southern part of that town the better.

The front is shifting, even our own position isn't permanent. Fate will decide who is to be ground under in this conflict.

During the night the Division took over another regimental sector further to the right. The enemy has retreated in places. My survey section has climbed a tall fir tree to help make a temporary flash ranging system. On the right flank two enemy units are said to have penetrated, each one hundred and fifty men strong. Some of them have been destroyed, but the greater part has gone into the woods to reinforce the partisans. Two squadrons of cavalry have come up from behind us and are trying to make contact with the enemy across our front line. Normally partisans don't attack fighting units, but we're obliged to take precautions. Of course we organise partisan-hunts and patrols go out regularly in the rear of our fighting echelons, but what's the good? Sweating and plagued by mosquitoes, our men fight their way through the dense undergrowth, they splash through the swamps and trail along the paths in the green twilight of the forests. They look exotic with machine-guns over their shoulders and cartridge belts slung round their necks, but they don't achieve much. In the woods the Russians are more than a match for them. Last night two characters from those cavalry squadrons rode along the main highway past the ammunition wagons of No. 11 Battery. Before our lads woke up and realised what was happening, they had long vanished.

In the early hours of this morning and towards midday there was a great noise of battle to the South-East, where the front is retreating.

It has become quieter. Preparations are going ahead for the change of position. Day after day the blue sky is filled with fighters. Hedge-hoppers with gleaming red stars roar over the tree-tops as if they want to brush them with their blue bellies. We fire as fast as we can, but the bastards are well armoured. This evening there was a regular traffic, crude-oilers flying hour after hour towards the rear area. It sounded as if they had opened an official air-channel. Since they were not dropping many bombs, they were presumably doing a large-scale supply flight.

10th of August, 1943. In the few pauses which now come my way I am trying to bring these pages up to date from the middle of July. Sometimes I get up and walk over to Wren, who stands further in the wood in the undergrowth. He turns his beautiful head, searches in my pocket, and gives me a reproachful nudge with his mouth if he doesn't find anything.

Yesterday evening there was lively air activity again. It went on hour after hour, but with the difference that this time Ivan was busy chucking bombs about. We couldn't even light a cigarette. A great part of the bombs plopped down in the swamp, but it's as if the tension which follows the whine in the air has not been released.

Yesterday evening there was a hit on No. 11 Battery limber position. They lost one man seriously wounded. At 1930 they moved to a better site. At 2200 the order came for us to change position in the morning. We have been on the road since 0600.

We are rolling without a pause down the great highway towards K. The vehicles travel at intervals of a hundred yards. They are stuck with branches and even the heads of the horses are decorated with greenery which nods in rhythm with their step. Aircraft are over us the whole time, both our own and the enemy's. The noise of their engines swells and dies, varies from high pitch to low as they circle round each other or try to get out of the flak puffs. The noise rises to a high, threatening scream when they bear down on the road. The smoke of bombs mingles with the mushrooms of our own shells which shoot up over the back of the woods and over whole quarters of the town. Round the horizon rise the silent, dark fires. There you have a picture of the scorched earth.

At 1430 we had our first rest. It was west of K. in a little wood. The stretches of cover on either side of the road made one big camp of troops in transit. Horses lay by the roadside, doubled up and with swollen bellies. The live ones shied away in terror.

On bad patches of the road there were the usual hold-ups. Horses tortured themselves dragging overloaded vehicles through the murderous sand, through deep swampy holes and over damaged corduroy roads. Once the long columns were at a complete standstill. When I had finally fought my way up to the head there was a miserable peasant's cart stuck in the mud. It was overloaded, of course. The poor horse stood working with his flanks, the sweat dripping from his belly. "Konye kaputt," the women wailed, holding a bunch of grass under his nose. Then even I got furious.

When our own drivers come to a difficult patch, they mount the saddle horse. A tap of the whip on the hind-quarters of the team, a few encouraging words, and the horses pull through.

It is all done quietly, in contrast with the noise and shouting of the pony columns. The Russians knock their horses up; and they have no idea how to handle our bigger horses at all.

At 1930 we turned off into some wooded country for a night's rest. It opened up after a few hundred yards, and we found ourselves at the edge of a park-like leafy wood, whose ancient trees overshadowed a thick lawn. A small steep slope led down to a clear stream. Dusk fell gently and slowly, and on the horizon the blue mixed with the red of the fires. We threw off our clothes and plunged into warm water, while the first stars rose above us. After all the noise and dust and heat, this hour was wonderful beyond belief.

CHAPTER XV

THE OLD FOREST

AT five o'clock we were off again. It was a bad road. The sand was so loose in parts that corduroy roads had to be laid. We went through fir trees by the side of the railway which leads to B. There were two open valleys where we had to cross some patches of marsh. Here the road, which was otherwise wide, narrowed to a track. The vehicles streamed down the slope and piled up before the defile. They were standing with their wheels at an angle on the corduroy road, which threatened to give way under the load. With wild shouts from the drivers the heavy covered wagons bumped and slid over the potholes and across the fascines which had been laid in the worst patches. The mud splashed up, the horses were breathing hard.

After watching all this in progress for a while, we took action. On the nearest hill were the ruins of a village. It was a matter of fifteen minutes to go there and bring back the first load of beams. Beam by beam—very soon we had made a firm surface. A grip on the spokes, a good shove and the first vehicles were on their way again. Slowly the jam started moving. We crossed a bridge which already hung drunkenly on its piers. Then we were at the new defence line. It was on the west side of the river valley—a bastion of logs and earth considerably taller than a man. Wiring parties were already at work in front of it, and in the foreground everything which could have been of use to the enemy had been destroyed.

In Ber . . . we turned off North-West. We passed through the gate of a ruined power-station which had once been linked with a big industrial plant. Then we drove across the bridge of a lock with a large reservoir and disappeared again into the woods. A high-tension wire ran on pylons through a clearing to some other works which lay hidden deep in the wilderness.

Once more we fought with alternating swamp and sand. The corduroy road ran through green puddles of stagnant water, where tree roots rose like luxuriantly overgrown bridges and islands. At other times the insidious swamp was concealed by a treacherous carpet of tempting green moss. Nobody but a fugitive or a criminal would have gone through here. Trees lay where they had broken down under storms or old age. There was absolute silence beneath the thick roof of leaves, a foetid smell hung lazily in the motionless air where only the mosquitoes were singing. A clearing opened, a village came into view, the sentries of the advance guard appeared.

The old forest, where we are now permanently bivouacked, hides us completely from view. With its firs and spruce, birches and beeches, the forest stretches over sand dunes and damp hollows. Deep down where the young trees struggle for light beside age-old trunks, there's a green twilight, a gold-and-emerald light which plays over ferns and moss and grasses. It's sometimes as if one were moving under glass or in the depths of sunny water. Our heavy boots sink noiselessly into the soft ground. Below the matt blueberry bushes shine the glossy lacquered leaves and smooth red fruit of the cranberries. It's a paradise of mushrooms. I don't know all their names and species, but I found yellow balls with ink-coloured dots which were almost hidden by the cushioning moss. There's a connoisseur among us who maintains they are truffles. Truffles—we ate them in the South of France, on the banks of the Lot, where the sun burned the walls of the house and our rooms had red-tiled floors.

Our foraging party has made a second visit to an area which has not been devastated by the present battle. The war went over it several times, the regular one and the bandits'. Few of the wooden villages are left standing. Now the smoke is going up from the last ruins. Where one summer has passed, the ground is already overgrown with grass. After two summers one can hardly find a trace, except here and there a weary, weather-worn fence and silver-bleached posts which mark a plot where the vegetation is different. The bridges are quickly rotting away, the paths are overgrown, wild carrots and lupins, pig-weed and pale wormwood reign supreme. Soon there will be only the tracks of the woodmen through the wilderness.

The party came back with three heavily loaded carts. They brought big dry potatoes with sand clinging to their thin skins, cabbages, beetroots, carrots, pumpkins and onions. At the field kitchen hangs a respectable leg of horsemeat. Among the trees are three cows, and the milk for Sunday pudding is slopping about in buckets.

There was said to be a deserted forester's house. We rode along narrow sandy tracks through glistening swamp and sun-filled clearings. Above us the wind was blowing in the tree tops, but down below there was only the creak of leather, the breathing of the horses and the thump of their hooves on the soft ground. When we dismounted and tied them up, the silence was complete. In the moss was a profusion of yellow *pfifferlinge*; they grew under the young firs and in the overgrown holes left by uprooted trees. The bag on my saddle was quickly filled. We rode through wild undergrowth where it was almost dark. Fat waterplants grew in the puddles, branches slapped in our faces, and the track was overhung with trees. Sometimes we had to crouch down on the horses' necks. Once we met a solitary despatch rider on horseback. Otherwise we encountered no one for four hours.

The forester's house lay in a little clearing. The wind blew through the open doors and broken windows. Laburnum nodded across the fence—the last echo of habitation. Once there had been some fields cut into the surrounding wood, but they had long gone to grass. The fences were falling down. The bugs in the large room had long ago starved and dried out in the crevices of the brown roof. I put a foot through the rotten moss-covered floor of the porch. However, there was something to be got here: the stout boards from the floor of the granary, the planks from the front of the attic, the doors and benches. It was worth sending a cart.

Aircraft were over us all through the night again. They were bombing B. Towards morning it started to rain. It grew into a cool, unfriendly day. Rain is no fun when you're in bivouacs. We fetched a roof from the village and fixed it between the trees. Even the pair of nuthatches which have nested close by, run a little less sprightly up the trees, and their calls reach us feebly through the rain. Only once was the sun reflected by the raindrops hanging from the branches, and then the smoke of the fires looked blue and transparent. We were feeling cold.

In the evening an aircraft dropped out of the sky in a steep hyperbola, faster and faster, with a wild blaze and a terrible howl from the engine. The spectacle ended abruptly. The noise was brutally silenced and there was a spreading glow of red. A night-fighter sang its silver song over the dark woods. But for all that, they were over us again later, and the earth trembled for hour after hour.

22nd of August, 1943. Yesterday night when the wet tent-roof glistened in the milky light, when in the darkness after the rain one could scarcely recognise the man opposite and there was nothing but the voice from the loudspeaker rushing by my ear, I felt for a while as if I had stepped out of myself and were completely alone. In my tiredness I felt overshadowed by the melancholy which overcomes us when we see the approach of the inevitable. Stripped of all hope, I sensed that there remained in me that final hardness like a thin steel spring, which I believe to be one of a man's greatest gifts.

Later an aircraft circled overhead, bringing something of a novelty in the way of propaganda. To our great amusement, it regaled us with music and a speech. The music was unbearable, the words inaudible. But the foreign cadence and unrestrained hatred of the words were clear. It seemed only proper that the plane finished by firing its machine-guns; it put the situation on a clear and honest basis again.

At 0700 eighty enemy bombers flew over on their way towards B. They appeared against the morning sky, squadron after squadron, in neat formation. It was an impressive sight and we listened expectantly. We were not disappointed.

At 0715 an O.P. signalled that six had been shot down in ninety seconds. The noise of engines and the short rasp of machine-guns went on for nearly an hour. We had no more time to listen to it. But afterwards forty-five enemy machines were on the ground. At eight o'clock the observers of No. 11 Battery were plastered by twenty rounds from Heavies which fell on their block house by the railway. Two hit the watch tower. The effect was almost nil. The observation continued. In the afternoon No. 10 Battery had one man killed by a solitary shell. The noise of battle was particularly strong to our left front. A light battery was pulled out of the line and sent over to the right, because we are expecting a big attack in the South. We follow the spotters' reports like a temperature chart. In the evening we moved into our new dug-out and took off our clothes for the first time in weeks.

When our horses came in from grazing last night they brought a black cow with them. She was trustful and affectionate, and we took a great fancy to her. When I went to the stables in the dusk, our drivers were standing in ambush. I stood leaning against a tree for a while, my eyes wandering over their faces. They were all turned towards me, and the evil temptation hung over us. I let them loose, and they didn't take long to get to work.

Soon the cow was hanging from a cross-beam far away in the undergrowth. We didn't know then that it had belonged to the Third. But we learnt it that night, because the search parties appeared. They combed our camp in every direction, and today they arrived armed and mounted, with dogs. They stood by the field-kitchen, watchful and suspicious. They sat there till evening, with tired eyes and worn-out faces. By then they were convinced of our honesty, despite Lieutenant R. having told them: "Have a good look round my old Headquarters Battery—they're specialists!"

But they weren't a match for us. When the suspicious Sergeant-Major arrived, I paraded the drivers and told them that any man who saw the cow belonging to the Third should catch her and notify them for old friendship's sake. It was the last straw, and the drivers thought they would have a stroke. It was a beautiful scene. When I dismissed them, they shot away, looking for somewhere quiet to release their pent-up laughter. Oh, what a wicked lot we were. But we had some noodle soup and there was fine yellow fat swimming on the top.

Yesterday a messenger arrived from Lieutenant R., asking us for two pints of milk. We were pleased to supply it—for old friendship's sake. This morning he came himself and we invited him to lunch. We happened to have a very good goulash, and plenty of it too. In the afternoon we had coffee with him. He was charming. And so we decided we were base, black souls of unfathomable meanness. We promised him milk whenever he wanted some, but we couldn't undo the crime.

We rode once more to the forester's house. My tough horse went like the devil. The branches which brushed our faces were heavily laden with glittering raindrops. At our feet lay the first red leaves, the grass was yellow and the fields had taken on a dull colour. So this summer too is nearing its end.

A week ago we began the construction of an artillery defence position designed as a second reserve line. Meanwhile we have had a visit from some brass-hats. The officer concerned painted a very black picture of the supply situation for the coming winter. It has been like that so many years now that it couldn't really upset us any more. But he gave us some further details which were more disturbing. Finally he said it was intended to send another hay-party to the rear so that we could at least secure some coarse feed. We swore. In the previous position we had collected mountains of course feed. Week after week fatigue parties had been mowing the Dnieper meadows. Now it was to start all over again. It's a job which takes away not only supply troops but also active men from the fighting units.

But there's nothing we can do about it. The additional needs of the unit and the difficulties of supply are too great. We're obliged to live off the land. Yesterday morning the Regiment sent a horse-catching party to the rear. Our battery supplied a sergeant and five men on a lorry. They were each given ninety rounds of ammunition and instructions to take the partisans' horses away from them. Lovely, isn't it?

Here we are situated in the part of the Eastern front which used to be the thickest partisan-territory, except for the Rokitno swamps and other charming neighbourhoods, of which I could tell the most astonishing tales. The partisans are a formidable weapon. Our struggle against them is outside any convention of war. Our hospital trains have had the Red Cross painted out because it only invited more than usually vicious attacks.

Today at 1600 we stood round the table with bitter faces. Then I passed by the men, who were just beginning to excavate our last dugout. They sat at the edge of the hole, their chins resting on the hands that held their spades. I motioned to them with the gesture that means 'chuck it up'. They got up, laughed a little and shrugged their shoulders. "We thought as much," they said, "but what the hell . . ." and went to their dugouts. Yes, that's how it is—anything but wonderful. If one looks at the black side, it's enough to break your heart. If one reacts in a healthy manner, as befits a soldier, it makes one sick. It's a waste of energy and good-will, a waste of this astonishing, tireless spirit of the troops, which even now, after four years of war, can still surprise you and almost excite your veneration. It's a waste for which a number of people should be soundly boxed on the ears. Not only have we completed all our summer stables, but we have also built underground shelters for sixty-five horses.

And what do the men say? They say—and one must consider how it shows their trustfulness—that it's probably being done to give us time to go back and build positions for the winter; that it's really quite a wise move because—it's true, isn't it?—there aren't any Russians round here . . . there can't be . . .

Chapter XVI

WE LIVE AT A MOMENT'S CALL

'This morning I found the first pieces of ice in the watering-bags.' I remember how I wrote that sentence a year ago. Today I repeat it—and at this moment the repetition seems frightening. The first sign of winter always comes too early. It only underlines the monotony of what is happening, and in that light all the things whose beauty I have tried to describe are paling. Are not the scenes of our Russian years eternally enacted on the same stage? When I close my eyes, even the change of scene seems small. The sights which have excited our wonder were seldom lovely. This country has no beauty, nothing to move or uplift us as other countries' beauties have moved us. Despite all the changes, our life here is so uniform that it's quickly measured out. Perhaps that's why, against this background, man's soul appears as something unique.

As I think of all this without bitterness—because it doesn't do to irritate oneself with bitterness—I am sitting in an easy chair and stretching out my legs. I don't really sit, I lie in it, as I used to lie in our big chairs at home. I am fully aware that it isn't 'done', not by an officer and the most junior lieutenant. Even if the Battery Commander doesn't notice it immediately, he must feel it subconsciously. It only needs to break through a thin layer to come within his consciousness. But I don't dream of changing my position. It's more important to see the fall of the light through the amber-coloured rum in the bottle, more important to slip out of uniform for a moment and not to feel my boots any more. What could be more important than that?

9th of September, 1943. I have been sitting over these pages for many days. I have written a great deal and it has given me much

195

to think about. Propaganda plays curious tricks on one, it coils like roots and branches round one's feet. The mind of nations seems to be like a photographer's plate which can be exposed according to one's whim.

Our mail delivery has got into a mess, not because of great military events, but because of the lack of them. It sounds paradoxical, but it's true. It's because we shouldn't really be here any more. The movement was fully worked out. At the first hint of alarm the boys at the base beat their usual hasty retreat to the new position. And now there they are, far away from us. In the meantime it became clear that there was no hurry, and we took our time. We dismantled slowly and kept finding jobs which could be done more thoroughly. The demolition squads set to work. For the moment we are in a state of suspended animation.

I too have sent a large number of vehicles to the rear, and with them the main baggage. The course of the epidemic among the horses is incalculable and I mustn't get immobilised. But nothing else is on. We live at a moment's call and enjoy our peace as long as we can. From day to day the sun shines more weakly through the trees. It doesn't give any real warmth any more. It's like a reflection of brass lying over the moss and young spruce. The shafts of light between the trees are no longer so painful to the eyes.

At eight o'clock we put torches to our dugouts. The flames roared out of the doors and window-shafts, and the smoke hung like a wall among the tall trees. We burned everything down to the last board.

Then we marched. At the level crossing by Kryutshek we halted for lunch. A railway-trolley was making a last slow journey down the line to the West. Two men sat aboard it throwing out explosives, two charges at a time and a length of fuse. Two Pioneers ran behind, wedging the explosive under the track and inserting the fuses. How they ran, the devils, and how the thin white jets of flame shot out of the earth! Lumps of iron hissed around and the bitter powder smoke blew over our heads. The road beside the railway was closed for an hour afterwards.

But that was only part of the destruction, a ridiculously small part. Every culvert, every defile was mined. For hundreds of yards through the woods the red charges were packed against the trees so that they could be thrown across the highroad with the least possible delay. The villages were on fire, burning with unbelievable fury. The heat barred our way. We went through at a gallop, shielding our faces against the rain of sparks. The vehicles had to make a detour. The clouds of smoke camouflaged us from enemy aircraft, and the noise of the explosions all round us was like a great battle.

In the suburbs of Briansk the smoke mingled with the yellow road-dust, shrouding us with a double cloak. The sun was red long before evening. It hung sick and thirsty above the march of destruction. Above the marching host, the clouds were lit from both sides. They made the finest, most sumptuous banners I ever saw, displaying war in all its terrible splendour. We saw houses in every stage of destruction: the blaze spurting like white magnesium-light from the windows, the first burst of red flame as it fought through clouds of black smoke, the triumphant dance of the Red Cock above the roofs.

We raced through the white heat of dying streets. As riders and horses ahead of me moved towards the walls of fire, the rifles slung across their backs looked like toys, like the lances of tiny devils on a silhouette. We saw houses collapse with a groan, the indescribable sight of old birches which, courted by the red fire-glow, shivered and wept at Death. Once again we rode through a forest of chimney-stacks which, rigid and angular, revolved before our gaze. Above the black carpet of the conflagration, they had the colour of Brussels lace. They rose in the moonlight like the stiff, lamenting hands of ghosts, and all around them was the foul, repulsive, half-choking smell of cold smoke.

Landscape of horror and death. Silent valleys surrounded from afar by blazing torches. Parachute-flares descending like Cyclopean eyes. Chrysanthemums of bombs, the gentle purling sheaves of fire which follow the sudden bloom.

Towards two in the morning the hurrying hooves of our horses thundered ahead of the battery across the bridge at Ograd. Beyond the ghostly river the horses jumped sideways, snorting as they saw the trenches of the new defence line. The white mist came up from the night-shrouded meadows, there was a movement of the dark sentries, the men of the advance guard fell on us with questions about their units.

Once again we spurred on our horses. Left and right, left and right. Ankle-deep sand, echoing cobbles, dark overgrown rivers of silent streets, hostile-hunched houses.

We drove along part of the new position. Along the road to the West moved a stream of refugees. It was fed by rivulets from the side-streets, directed by a handful of police, covered by the dust stirred up by thousands of feet. What a trek of misery! Lord have mercy. Those wretched carts, drawn by cows and small ponies. Sometimes the people still fought against it, instinctively, like animals. But they got rough treatment. "Where are we going?"—"Go to the devil, I don't know. Get moving! You too. Just keep going West. Hurry up, we have no time!" Wherever the front lays its hand, all other life is stifled. It throws up a wave which reaches far beyond it. The lower town has already changed its face. The houses are only stage properties serving new purposes. Or is it only our eyes which see them differently?—they appraise the town, across the foreground of the new position, and they find it good.

I went into the gardens on the nearby roadside, gathering tomatoes and flowers. I put a bunch of velvet-brown stars into a slim vase and set the table in the porch facing the street. There's a little bench where you can sit in the evenings looking towards the South and West. It lies full in the sunshine. In its struggle with the daylight the dusk makes the colours seem deeper and more glowing. I feel so happy being alone in my own way, happy to the very tips of my fingers.

A few moments ago, at 2130, the order came to march on at 0600. Alas for this position, this wonderful line on the heights West of the town and the Bolva, with the river as a defence and a field of fire such as we have never had before. Alas for Briansk, from whose tall buildings I watched the suburbs burning. I would have liked to see it whole and in the day—we would have been happy to defend it.

Before four o'clock the night was over. It was cold in the dark small hours. We were still cold when we had already crossed the Desna and had put the town behind us. Soon I was motoring ahead to scout for rest areas. Motoring, mark you, because we were marching on the *Rollbahn* and I didn't see any reason to maltreat my seat when there were command cars to thumb.

I was again riding in a car in the evening and fetched up in a village built on both sides of a small valley. That's where we are now. Inside, the houses are better than they look. Often they consist of one tiny room—typical Russian peasants' houses, just a single room built round a stove. But they are clean, these rooms, and the people are lively and approachable. It's a friendly place. Admittedly, down in the valley there are the burnt-out vehicles of our workshop-company; a few days ago the partisans came, four hundred of them. You can't see into anyone's soul. But what does it matter?

Corn-sheaves are piled in front of the houses. A herd of cows comes trotting into the valley against the setting sun; they're enveloped in a cloud of saffron dust. From the houses on the slopes women and children come calling them with clear cries. We have had a wash, we feel good. We are content.

4th of September, 1943. We rolled along the great highway which cuts across the valleys and hills, straight as a Roman legionary road. From far away you could see the sheets of dust blowing, marking the road like a swathe in the open, treeless country. We were marching so well that I unpacked my guitar. We marched along singing, behind the leading vehicles, and we were singing as we crossed the riverside meadow where our road turned off. Perhaps it surprised people. The last battery had just crossed the bridge when a squadron of fighter-bombers wheeled in and lowered their noses at the defile which led down to the river. As they flew off they spattered us with bullets. In the batteries there were only some minor casualties and a little damage, but at such moments it is almost impossible to hold the horses.

In the afternoon we reached Shukova which was our operational area. As we went to tactical headquarters, the sun was sinking in a golden smoke. The golden background of a gothic altar painting could hardly have equalled the luminosity of the horizon with the tall firs in the foreground, nor the light which flowed like smoke round the villages and woods.

When I arrived with Wolf and Jean Braun at the airfield, the infantry were in extended line preparing to attack. We joined up with them. We went across the landing field. The enemy was dug in amid the scrub and in folds of ground on the edge. We advanced quickly and took some foxholes and craters on the perimeter. From there we could overlook the depression beyond. Two hundred yards ahead we saw the smoke of a mortar which was still firing at us, and we spotted the enemy infantry who were firing at our left-hand neighbours. They were sitting in two deep anti-tank ditches. I brought down the fire of the whole battery. The enemy withdrew to the village, setting fire to houses and bales of straw to cover his retreat. Wireless communication went excellently. Franz and Jean were hopping behind me from hole to hole with stick aerials in their hands, headsets round their necks, morse-keys in their pockets. They set up and dismantled every ten minutes throughout the attack.

We took three patches of scrub and part of the first anti-tank ditch. The enemy only retreated from the ditch when his flank was attacked by the battalion on our right. We captured the second ditch and the edge of the village, and now had the cover of the smoke for ourselves. Here the attacking units collided, attracted by the desperate resistance of the Russian infantry. Some of the Russians were fighting in the captured uniforms of German flak-troops. I was lying on top of a dugout behind which the commander of one of the attacking groups had taken cover from an anti-aircraft gun; enveloped by the smoke I tried to locate this damned squirt. The enemy artillery became more lively, field guns and Stalin organs began to plaster us. In the dugout below me a child was crying.

We had advanced beyond the day's objective. We sorted out the units and went back to the position allotted us on the high ground round the perimeter. Meanwhile the enemy had ranged his guns. We went down on our stomachs once more. Franz and Jean were swearing, complaining that their backs were black and blue from carrying the set. The infantry dug in on the landing field. It was getting towards evening. I was supposed to range a barrage, and the plate battery was exhausted. The Russians tried a counter-attack but were pinned down by our fire. We joined up with a spotter and took it in turns to use the same auxiliary set. I ranged the barrage by the light of the fires.

Only then could we think wearily of finding some shelter and also of the fact that for the last two hours our rations and blankets had been waiting for us somewhere back in the wood. We found the narrow shaft of a bomb store. There we crept in, together with the spotters and a few infantrymen. The moon came up like a huge red ball, Franz and Jean went nearly three kilometres across the landing field to look for our cart.

It was almost midnight when they returned, having picked their way through wire and craters, rubble and stacks of bombs. In the interval we had found a stove, bent some pipes to fit it, and made a fire. The silver moon was gently veiled. There was frost

on the stubble and the shallow pits of the infantry—but we had
a fire. The bullets whistled across the field—but we had three foot
of earth over our heads. Our horse stood behind the shelter. Jean
gave him a box of fodder to keep him from lifting his head.

A little after three o'clock the order came through to change
position. At 0345 we marched back. It was still dark. Once
again we searched for our way through rubble and wire and
pulverised concrete. We could see the dead in the scrub, the
fallen horses and the shattered vehicles on the road, the heaps
of torn equipment. Our palates were dry from smoking and
tiredness. Between walls, and through the gaping windows of
shelled buildings, we could see the fire-red morning sky. It
turned yellow, and rain began to fall. When it hung grey and
low and the land was as if it were wrapped in cold poultices, we
gave up. The roads were like sticky porridge. The grass was
covered with a white sheen. In some of the fields the potato tops
were still standing, brown and faded. We were soaked to the
skin, dirty and tired, when we found ourselves billets in some
houses in Malyi Salyn.

Tomorrow we are to move into position. According to the
Wehrmacht communiqué, the enemy has begun the expected
large-scale attack west of Yelnya. The three cavalry regiments
have become divisions.

I am sitting on a paliasse in the open air, waiting for the order
to go forward on liaison duty. The infantry-gun shells are
twittering over the heights from the East. Four tanks are breaking
through across the railway line in the North. The shells on No. 11
Battery creep slowly towards them, till the muzzle-flashes of
their guns stand out red in the clouds of the shellbursts. They
turn away clumsily.

We go forward and climb down the slopes towards the railway.
Tanks and anti-tank guns are firing at individual men. We lie
for a long time behind the cover of a little scarp and feel our way
from bush to bush. The bushes are sparse. We are clearly

silhouetted on the ridge. It's a clear, warm late-summer day. The fields of buckwheat glow rust-red in the sun. Over in the enemy's lines another village is burning. We drop into the valley of a little stream, where we find a telephone line running towards the enemy. Soon we are eating the daily bread of the infantry, high-pitched bursts of machine-gun fire, howling high-velocity shells, and slow, heavy fellows with a deep bass humming which shake the earth. The powder fumes blow across in lazy waves. At last we end up at Lieutenant Illner's. He is sitting by the stream, washing his feet: "It's eight days since I last got out of my boots. It's a nice quiet moment. . . ."

At 1730 we got the order over the wireless: "Back at once." At 1830 Jean Braun was waiting for us at the edge of the village. He led out the horse from the dip where he had tethered it. Half an hour later we were in the village where the gun position was. The batteries were ready to move off. Headquarters had left already. Far around us the sky was red. It was almost night. A girl was leaning from a window. She recognised me; I had been billeting for the battery. "You not go," she said softly. "Oh, *panyenka*, what do you know about war!" Wren was already saddled. We rode off after the battery, overtaking dark columns. The heavy binoculars clattered and bumped on my belt. We reached the battery.

We march. It is cold. Midnight comes. The moon sails through silver clouds. The parachute-flares shine brightly like constellations. Somewhere bombs whistle. I take out my guitar: "*Weisst Du, wieviel Sternlein stehen . . .—Horch, was kommt von draussen rein! . . .*" Franz looks pale and sick, with deep lines round his mouth and eyes. He has a temperature. I feel as if my stomach had been pumped out and as if I had swallowed salt water. I have eaten one slice of bread since midday. The cart fell on its side, everything is dirty.

Let it go, it doesn't matter. It's still too cold to eat while we're marching. Let's have another song, let's smoke another cigarette, then we won't notice it so much. Slowly they fall asleep on the wagons and in the saddles. Von R. has to wake up a lorry driver who lies snoring over his wheel. For kilometres behind us the column was at a standstill. At 0400 we reach our billets.

Two days later Helmut Pabst was killed in action.

Russia, 17th April, 1942.
(Last Will)

Dear Parents,

I have only one anxiety: how is it possible to ease your pain? What can I do to soften the blow which no longer hurts me, but only you? I will gather all my strength to entreat you:

My life was not completed, but it was fulfilled. It was fulfilled by your love, and it was so rich that I can only thank you again and again. Even if the other life in which I wanted to do my work as a man was hardly begun, this first life was utterly fulfilled and consummated, the one which you gave me and which you guarded, my Father, my Mother.

I loved you very much.

If you want to erect a small figure in my memory in the garden, let it not be with a grand gesture nor anything perpetuating sorrow. It might be a boy who smiles a little, who radiates harmony and reconciliation, or perhaps a young man who rests at peace with himself, so that my heart could become attached to it, not turned away from the world, but open to everything beautiful.

Farewell, I loved you very much.